UNROBING
THE
SHAME

Debbie & Tim Shultz

Dedication

We dedicate this book to Thomas and Abigail, our children who are safe in the arms of Jesus, who we long to embrace one day.

Acknowledgments

We thank God for transforming our lives with His unconditional love, setting us free from the shackles of secrecy and shame, and for anointing this book for His good purposes.

We thank our amazing parents, siblings, and children for extending grace and forgiveness as we unveiled our secret, and for loving and supporting us throughout our healing journey.

We thank our son, Christian, for patiently coaching us through the writing and publishing process, for designing both covers, and for being our biggest cheerleader throughout this writing adventure.

We thank every single person who prayed diligently for us as we embarked into this unknown territory of book writing. Your prayers strengthened, encouraged and carried us through the difficult times.

We thank First Step Women's Center board and staff for recognizing the need for abortion recovery and for investing financially into God's healing mission.

Contents

Foreword

The Bible says, "They triumphed over him by the blood of the Lamb and by the word of their testimony…" Revelation 12:11

In their book, *Unrobing the Shame,* Debbie and Tim Shultz not only overcome the enemy, they completely conquer and defeat him! He has no power here!

I have heard their story many times over the past ten years of our ministry together and it never, ever gets old.

First of all, this precious couple defeated Satan's plan to destroy their relationship. Some statistics quote as high as 80% of all couples who experience an abortion together never stay together. The pain and shame are simply too heavy to carry through a marriage relationship.

Many couples who are able to get through this heartbreak might stop with that and rightly consider it a victory. Debbie and Tim did not stop at one devil defeat! They followed the call of God on their lives and went far beyond that first victory step. Together they spearheaded a ministry in Illinois that God has used for the saving of many, many lives. This new book goes one more mighty step and offers their story to the world!

Persons who struggle with the pain of a past abortion often feel alienated. With the overall cultural message they receive that abortion is a perfectly reasonable and often a best choice, if they regret their decision, they conclude that something must be wrong with them. Within our subculture of faith, they fear they will be judged and condemned for taking the life of their own innocent child. The church has a wonderful opportunity to reach out to those women and men turning to us for redemption, restoration, and freedom in Christ. When we extend mercy and compassion to those impacted by abortion, we participate in Christ's promise that He will heal the brokenhearted and bind up their wounds. (Ps. 147:3)

Abortion wounds the hearts of women and men.

Abortion wounds the heart of the nation.

Abortion wounds the heart of God.

The miracle of redemption shared in this book will open the floodgates of God's healing grace and pour out a soothing balm of freedom and hope. This book is for every woman or man who has endured the devastating shame and loss of a past abortion and those who love them.

I encourage you to read it for you and read it for those God places in your path who need this heartbreak to be healed.

It blesses me beyond words to have been a small part of God's huge plan for their lives through *Surrendering the Secret* and the many ministry adventures we have shared together.

In His Grip for Eternal Life,

Pat Layton, Author, *Surrendering the Secret*: Healing the Heartbreak of Abortion (Lifeway, 2009)

Introduction

Debbie

For years, people have encouraged us to write this book. People who have been moved and touched by our story of brokenness and redemption. People who found courage to walk their own unique healing journey as a result of our transparency. People who believe our story could ignite transformation in other heartbroken women and men.

For years, we gravitated toward writing our redemption journey, believing God was leading us in this endeavor.

For years, we put it off.

In 2019, God pinpointed to me and Tim that it was time to relinquish my everyday responsibilities as Executive Director of First Step Women's Center, and singularly focus on abortion recovery ministry full-time.

As a result of this life-changing shift, we seized the moment, and captured this window of opportunity...it was time.

The main purpose of this book is to reveal how the abortion decision we made together in 1986 destructively impacted our lives, and to elaborate on how God's extravagant love, grace, forgiveness and healing saturated our lives since then.

For those readers who are struggling with past abortion decisions, our desire is that you will be empowered with courage to discover the struggles and victories engraved within these pages. Courage to take the next step, to explore the life-giving resources listed in the back of this book and reach out for help. Courage to trust God through your healing process.

For those readers who may not have personally experienced abortion, you most likely know someone who has. A family member, friend, co-worker, neighbor, student or peer. Our hope is that this book will be lovingly shared with that someone.

We believe it is important to include both of our perspectives, female and male, to give our readers the inside look into the devastation abortion brings to both women and men, as well as the transformation we each experienced. So, we wrote in this conversational format.

All names mentioned have been changed, except for the names of our family members.

This book is segmented into three sections:

Section I spans the first 30 years of our lives. We share about our childhood years, how we met, what led up to the pregnancy and abortion decision, and how that decision impacted our lives.

Section II highlights the aspects of our lives during the next decade that led to the dramatic reconstruction of our identities, our marriage and our family, as well as stories that demonstrate God's abundant favor and blessings, even while still hiding our sin.

Section III offers hope for each one of us, diving into God's word, revealing His truths and promises for healing.

Tim

We share powerful testimonies throughout these pages that may seem strange in a book about healing after abortion. We highlight those in hopes that you are encouraged to know that God blesses all of us, even when we don't deserve it. Because His blessings are not based on who we are, but on who He is. His true character as our heavenly Father can't help but manifest blessings upon His children.

Also, we mention specific times when God spoke to us. When we make this reference, it doesn't mean we heard God speak audibly. It means that we believe the Holy Spirit impressed this upon our spirits in a way that was clearly not our own thinking.

We don't consider ourselves to be special by hearing from God. We are simply a couple growing in our relationship with Him and dedicating our lives to seeking after and pleasing Him.

Thank you for taking time to read this little book. Our desire is that it glorifies God for transforming our lives and launches many forward, to take the next step toward our Healer. Even if one person is empowered, our mission has been accomplished.

I.

The First 30 Years

1

How It All Began

July 1986 - Vicksburg, Mississippi

Debbie

"Congratulations, you're pregnant!" said the young nurse behind the counter.

Struggling to hold back my tears, my fiancé and I rushed out the clinic doors, into the sweltering heat, where I collapsed into his arms, weeping. With Tim's arm around me, my sobs continued as he guided me toward his truck and opened the passenger door.

I slid across the vinyl seat, ignoring the burn on the back of my bare legs, and dropped my head into my hands as the reality of those words hit hard. My mind swirled.

How did this happen?
I trusted Tim to protect us.
What is everyone going to think?
Our families.
Our pastors.
Our friends at church and school.
I could lose my scholarship.

We're only 20.
What are we going to do?

I was the good girl. The girl who others looked up to. Who didn't do drugs, drink, or party. Who went to church and stayed out of trouble. A leader and honor roll student. Who committed to save sex for marriage.

This wasn't supposed to happen to me.

You see, I grew up in a stable home, with loving parents and two sisters, one older and one younger. We lived in a modest home in an average-sized town, Galesburg, Illinois, in the 1970's. I was awkwardly shy, but playing outside with the boys in my neighborhood brought me out of my shell.

Regardless of the season (or the harsh winter weather), my favorite pastimes involved football, baseball, tag, riding bikes, basketball, matchbox cars in the gravel driveway, climbing trees, running races, gathering earthworms for our next fishing trip, catching fireflies, even defending others from bullies.

I tried taking piano lessons, but the lure of the fresh outdoors air squelched my commitment to be inside practicing.

I guess you could say I was a tomboy to my core.

It was in 4th grade that my love for basketball began as I won a free-throw shooting contest at my school. My family traveled to another town for a regional competition, where I earned my first trophy. My mom says they didn't even know I could shoot a basketball!

At Little League baseball try-outs, my strong throwing arm impressed the coaches when I was 11 and 12 years old, ensuring me a spot on the roster. I carry fond memories of those humid summer nights at O.N. Custer park. With my parents cheering from the bleachers, I remember chasing down high pop flies just before they hit the ground, sliding into second base just under the tag or striking out our opponents with my unorthodox pitching style. With dirt on my face and sweat trickling down my cheeks, I fit in as one of the boys.

When I turned 13, there wasn't a lot of sports opportunities for girls. I played a little softball, but it just wasn't the same. I wanted to try out for the football team, but my mom was afraid I would get hurt. Moms are so smart...thanks Mom!

Organized sports at junior high school opened up a whole new world for me. I learned basic volleyball skills, ran track and developed my budding basketball talents. My athletic nature and court sense allowed me to excel and lead our teams to winning seasons.

Catching the eye of the high school coaches, I played at the Varsity level my sophomore year. As an underclassman, not everyone was happy that I was playing ahead of them. But, my quiet personality kept me focused on my skills and pleasing my coaches, staying out of the drama.

As a three-sport athlete - volleyball, basketball, and softball - there wasn't much down time, but I thrived when competing, pushing myself harder and harder to be the best I could be. Determined would be a good word to describe me. Or some would say strong-willed.

I thank God for my parents and sisters, who were always there for me throughout all of my endeavors, supporting and cheering me on, giving me a strong foundation to build the rest of my life on.

Besides sports and school, our family was very involved at our small, local church. Whenever the doors were open, we were there. Back then, we had to wear a dress every Sunday. Easter involved a frilly hat, socks, and tiny purse. Ugh! The tomboy in me hated that! But I wanted to please my mom, so

I went with it.

My spiritual foundation was formed through our strong family values, mealtime devotions, and prayer times. along with the kids' activities, classes and programs at our church. I'm thankful for a mother who prayed constantly (and still does), as well as the timeless Bible basics I learned from the dedicated teachers and pastors who served our church so well.

The week-long summer camp with our Youth Group at Camp Epworth in northern Illinois created a memorable impression on my young spirit. While the sports activities and competitions were a thrill for me, and new friendships were made, I specifically remember being asked by the camp pastor to spend Time Alone With God (TAWG). Each of us found a quiet place…mine was under a tree on the out-skirts of the camp grounds.

It was in those still moments, leaning against that tree on a hot summer day, when the tears fell, and I re-dedicated my life to Christ. I prayed to invite Jesus into my heart when I was younger, but, this defining moment, as a young teenager, was different. It solidified my relationship with Him, as I surrendered my strong will, and dedicated my life to serving Him.

Later, as an upperclassman, our Youth Group students voted me to be one of the student leaders, and other area Youth Groups invited me to speak to their students about how to live a life for Jesus, while facing the temptations and challenges of being a teenager.

As graduation neared, I dreamed of diving around the volleyball court on a competitive college team and pursuing a degree to fulfill my desire to be an Athletic Director and Coach. I was recruited by our local school, Carl Sandburg Junior College, to join their volleyball and basketball programs, and signed a letter of intent to attend the fall of 1984. Little did I know that my life was about to change forever.

Tim

Growing up as the youngest of eight children, five boys and three girls, no matter what, I will always be my Momma's baby. I grew up between Tennessee and Illinois, the son of a Spirit-filled preacher. With seven older siblings, I was an uncle three times before I was born!

There are eight years between me and my next sibling, my brother, Jim. My oldest sibling, brother Ray, is 21 years older than me. My mom likes to say I was the only one of the eight she and Dad planned! Whatever the reason, I'm glad she chose life one more time.

Living in Tennessee as a kid on a 300+ acre farm, I was free to roam the woods and investigate my surroundings. I learned at an early age how things worked on the farm and where our food came from. Not only about our meat from the beef we raised or chickens or wild game we hunted, but also about the garden and all the delicious bounty that comes from hard work in the field.

We would take yearly blackberry- and raspberry-picking trips so Mom could make us delicious jelly to last the year round. We would collect wild nuts and mushrooms and lots of other bounty from the woods.

Each season of the year, Dad would show us things in nature that could help us in some way. Things like taking a small piece of a green birch branch, breaking it off and roughing it up on the end like a tooth brush, then brushing our teeth.

In my early years, I went to a little four-room school house in the country. It was first through eighth grades, with two grades in each room. There was one big room for lunch, which had a stage at one end for whole school assemblies.

Those humble beginnings I do not regret or dismiss. I am thankful for the life skills and understanding about how life works. I consider it a blessing to have that knowledge.

Being a preacher's kid was like what you might think. We were at church all the time. If Jesus was coming back, Dad wanted Him to find us at church. You could say I literally cut my teeth on the church pews. I'm talking old school church. Southern, spirit-filled brush arbor meetings and tent revivals…old camp meeting church.

I remember a time I was about seven years old at a Wednesday night church service. As the service lingered on into the night with extended altar and prayer time, it was hard to stay awake. At times, I was allowed to lay on the back pew and rest, often falling asleep, and this night was one of those times.

I fell asleep listening to my father's voice praying for someone, and the next thing I knew, I'm waking up in a completely dark church! I remember standing at the big glass exit doors, scared and all by myself, thinking, *Did Jesus come back and everyone is gone but me?*

Right then, Mom and Dad came squealing around the corner in the car coming back to get me. Mom thought Dad picked me up and Dad thought Mom picked me up. Classic. There were no car seats for the kids back then, so no car seat to check. I can tell you I was one happy little boy when Dad unlocked that door, gave me a hug and told me he was sorry. I was happy not just because Mom and Dad came back for me, but because I didn't miss Jesus.

Growing up, I witnessed signs and wonders, healings and the true love and power of a living Savior, Jesus Christ. At an early age I accepted Christ as my Savior. My relationship with Jesus and my upbringing would be the foundation for my future.

As I started coming of age around 6th grade, I guess it started to become obvious that I was going to be a pretty big kid (yes, I wore husky jeans). Everyone encouraged me to try basketball and running track.

I remember our old garage with a nine-foot basketball hoop on the front. As my coordination started to develop, I was able to run and jump and push myself off the garage wall under the hoop and rise up and dunk the ball, pretending to be like Dr. J, who I liked to watch on TV.

In 7th grade, I was six feet tall, 170 pounds and showing some raw talent. Just as the basketball season was getting started, we moved to Illinois, to a small town near Galesburg, in the winter of 1978-79. After the move and getting settled in, I started my fifth different school in six years. Yes, we moved around a lot as Dad chased after the Lord, always willing to say yes to Jesus, but I don't resent it.

Starting my 8th grade year, I was 6'2" and 180 pounds. I was a sponge soaking up all the coaching I could get. I was introduced to football and as a bigger than average running back in 8th grade, you can imagine how much fun I had! For a small town in farm land U.S.A., we thought we were pretty good. That 8th grade group of young men won the triple crown that year: conference champs in football, basketball and track.

As I transitioned into high school, I started on the Junior Varsity basketball team as a freshman and dressed Varsity. I also ran Varsity track and received my Varsity letter that year. As a sophomore, I started Varsity football, basketball and track, receiving most valuable player for football. Along with that success, over the next two years came many more accolades and achievements. I was living on the high of fame and notoriety, doing whatever I wanted, and living for the next newspaper article telling me how great I was.

Before my senior year, my mom and dad moved from Illinois back to the south, to Mississippi, to pastor a church in Cleveland. I lived with one of my older brothers in the same small town.

As my senior year was coming to a close, I struggled to define what was next in my life. I considered going to school, joining the military or entering the work force.

June 1984

Debbie

One of the honors I received during my high school career was the invitation to play in the Pizza Hut All-Star Basketball game, just a week after graduation. Male and female athletes from around the county were invited to play, forming guy and girl East and West teams.

A few weeks before, I met a guy at the city league softball field where I worked as a scorekeeper, who introduced me to his brother, Tim Shultz. Tim lived about 8 miles from Galesburg, and said he was invited to play in the All-Star game too. He asked if I was going with anyone to the Honor Banquet, and I said yes.

Arriving at the banquet, Tim approached our table, with every seat filled with family and friends. He asked who my date was, and I quickly realized that he had asked me to be his date for the banquet! I was going with family and friends...not a date, ha! Just a little insight as to how naive I was.

The All-Star game was the next night. I showed up in my East uniform, sporting #30, the same number I'd been wearing my entire high school career. Our girls East team won handily, then I settled in to watch the boys. To my surprise, Tim was also wearing the East #30 jersey! He later confirmed that he wore #30 throughout his high school basketball career too. That one seemingly insignificant coincidence created an instant bond.

Tim showed off his talent by dunking in warm-ups. To his dismay, a metal piece on the rim peeled back a thick layer of skin on his middle finger! With a bandaged shooting hand, he impressed me (and my dad) with his hustle and aggressive play on the court, leading his team to a victory.

Tim

My brother had just introduced me to the pretty young lady from the nearby town, at the softball field where she was the scorekeeper. When we discovered we were both playing in the area All-Star basketball game, being the bold, full of myself self, I asked if she was going to the Honor Banquet with anyone and she said yes. Totally shot me down.

At the time I didn't think much about it. My mind was on my future, what I was going to do next, and getting ready for the game.

After the Honor Banquet, I was pleased to find out the someone she went with was her family.

I realized I had seen that scorekeeper before. As soon as I got home, I broke out my keepsake books a friend of the sports program, a fan of mine, had put together. He gave me two scrapbooks of my senior year...one for football and one for basketball/track. All newspaper clippings of me and only me.

Little did I know that in one of those books was my life helpmate. Right in the middle of my book...I'm telling you, right there, smack dab in the middle of my book, was a newspaper clipping of Debbie Roberts, Western Big 6 Conference Player of the Year! That got my attention. God had a plan!

The games were great fun. I still have my Pizza Hut All Star game plaque and my blue East, number 30 jersey. Debbie played great, scoring 32 points! I did ok, scoring 16 points, including a finger roll over the rim, breakaway lay-up! (Too bad I'll never jump that high again until I get to Heaven.)

After the game I tried to find Debbie, thinking, *Any girl with a jump shot better than mine is worth finding!* But, she had already left.

I wanted to call her, but I couldn't remember her dad's first name. I got the phone book out and our new push-button phone, opened up to "Roberts" and started calling. I called every "Roberts" in the book, each time asking, "Is Debbie there?" But the answer was always "No."

Finally, someone answered the phone and said, "Yes." My response was "Really?" I couldn't believe I had found her and that she was going to talk to me!

That call was the beginning of our story together. I'm glad I didn't give up after Albert Roberts or Bill Roberts or Charles Roberts or Don Roberts. I thank Jesus I made it to Lester Roberts, because that's where I found my All-Star!

Debbie

Impressed by Tim's pursuit of me, we began talking on the phone every day, and seeing each other as much as possible. I call Tim my Knight in Shining Armor; however, he wasn't riding a horse, but a 1982 Kawasaki motorcycle! He didn't own a car at that time…just a motorcycle.

You can imagine my parents' concerns (especially with bitter cold Illinois winter just months away) watching their 18-

year-old daughter riding off in the sunset on the back of a motorcycle! But, they fell in love with Tim, just like I did. His magnetic, fun personality captured my heart, as the summer months turned to fall.

That August, we both attended Carl Sandburg College, diving into college life and a busy volleyball schedule. Next came basketball. Tim played on the men's team, but injured his shoulder during the pre-season, and was forced to quit the team.

He decided to move to Mississippi after Christmas to live with his parents and to find work.

Our women's team fought through a tough season and post-season, landing a spot at the National Junior College Athletic Association tournament in Senatobia, Mississippi, in February! Not only was I elated to earn that honor as a team, but the location was just hours from where Tim was living, so I would get to see him!

The day before our first tournament game (just 9 months after we met), Tim arrived at our beautiful hotel. He got down on one knee, held up a beautiful solitaire ring and asked me to marry him! Wow was I excited!

Now, my coach on the other hand...he was not. He didn't want me to be distracted from playing my best in the biggest game of my life to that point. He wasn't disappointed, as I played more focused and determined than ever, leading our Lady Chargers to a victory!

After spending his money on my ring, Tim couldn't afford to stay in the costly hotel our team stayed in, so he slept in his parents' van in the hotel parking lot. His humility, love and dedication to our relationship caused my love for him to deepen.

After the tournament, heading back to Illinois was hard,

and maintaining a long-distance relationship was even harder. No cell phones or FaceTime back in the day, so staying connected was difficult.

Summer Adventure - 1985

Debbie

Missing each other terribly, Tim moved back to Galesburg that spring, scratching out a living on his own, as a 19-year-old man.

He found an upstairs apartment to rent from a retired railroad man, C.B., and his wife, Betty, who embraced us and quickly became like family. We shared meals together, Tim helped with household chores, and any other work that needed to be done, in exchange for rent. Tim and C.B. quickly developed a strong friendship.

Their love for motorcycles and the outdoors led C.B. and Betty to make plans for Tim and I to join them on their annual summer vacation to the mountains of Colorado, covering most of our expenses.

They purchased a pop-up camper and two dirt bikes for us to borrow for this 10-day adventure. Excitement built as we loaded up our supplies and hooked up the camper to Tim's 1979 Chrysler Cordoba.

Tim grew up riding motorcycles, dirt bikes, and four wheelers on the farm. Not used as toys or entertainment, but as tools to help wrangle cows, pull wagons, and haul hay.

I had never ridden motorcycles, or taken a trip like this, but the thrill of a new adventure drew me into saying yes.

Following behind C.B.'s truck and full-sized camper, we sped along the highways, toward our mountain destination.

Seeing the incredible Rocky Mountains on the horizon still

many miles away was a beautiful sight. Having only seen mountains one other time, at first, they looked like clouds. But as we got closer, the majestic beauty of these formations was breath-taking.

After stopping at a grocery store at the bottom of Pike's Peak for food and supplies, we began the ascent to our Pike National Forest camp site. Weaving our way around twists and turns, ever so slowly pulling our cargo behind us, Tim's Cordoba struggled to make the climb. Fearing the engine would over-heat as we pushed the car beyond its original purpose, I prayed a silent prayer for God's help and protection.

After turning onto a dirt road and being surrounded by forest on every side, we rounded the last curve and, with a sigh of relief, rolled into our camp site. We finally made it!

My excitement grew as we set up camp. We opened the camper, arranged our personal belongings, tucked the food away in Betty's refrigerator, strung our clothesline between two trees to hang wet towels and clothing, and gathered sticks and wood for the campfire.

I stopped to take in the moment. Inhaling a deep breath of fresh mountain air, I thanked God for creating such a magnificent landscape. For giving Tim and I this opportunity of a lifetime. I felt at peace and stood in awe of the beauty around me.

As the sun began to set, our campfire kept us warm against the chill of the air. Stretching out our legs toward the hot blaze kept our toes warm inside our boots. Lounging around that campfire night after night, listening to the crackle of the burning wood, mesmerized by the dancing flames is one of my fondest memories.

Exhausted from the long day and a half trip, we fell into bed, and drifted off to sleep to the sounds of the forest creatures' symphony.

Sunrise came too soon, but the excitement of the adventure awaiting us (and the delicious smell of bacon!) overcame our weariness.

After a hearty breakfast, Tim gave me a quick riding lesson, then we gassed up our dirt bikes and hit the trails.

How exhilarating it was to ride up and down the trails, zigzagging through the trees, climbing higher up the mountain.

We came to a clearing overlooking a thousand foot drop off into the canyon below. With the high noon sun on our faces, we basked in the beauty before us. Cliffs of rugged rock on one side, trees and brush in every shade of green imaginable lining the mountainside. The clear, brilliant blue sky gave us a birds-eye view of the landscape for miles and miles. It was simply breath-taking.

After taking mental snapshots, we hopped on our bikes and headed back toward camp, hungry for hotdogs and smores over the open fire.

Riding for hours and hours on rough terrain and at that elevation was exhausting. But we loved it! We thrived in that environment together, being challenged physically and living in the wild outdoors.

As my confidence grew in my dirt biking abilities, one day I pushed my limits a little too far. There were some paved paths, actually very narrow roads, that we biked on a few times.

As I neared a curve in the road, I realized I was going too fast and tried to slow down before hitting a patch of loose gravel. But it was too late.

My rear tire skidded through the pea gravel, sliding the bike out from under me, leaving me with a gravel burn on my legs and a bruised ego. Embarrassed by my rookie mistake and feeling bad about damaging C.B.'s bike, I pushed it back to camp and vowed not to ride anymore.

Tim lovingly reassured me that everyone makes mistakes and that's just part of the learning process. He didn't belittle me or make fun of me. Rather, he patiently encouraged me, revealing his caring and understanding demeanor. His true character shone through, stamping a lasting impression upon my heart.

Tim

About halfway into our trip, C.B. arranged for me to take a day ride with the local trail-riding pro, C.B.'s friend.

It was a gorgeous day as we started our trip about ten in the morning. As we rode the isolated trail for several hours through the mountains, we approached a deep creek crossing. My new friend and guide surveyed the crossing, picked the best route he thought we could cross, and started through the water. Riding his new 1985 Honda 650cc Enduro with its high suspension, he made it safely across but not without some work and very skillful riding.

As he came out of the water on the other side, he parked his bike and encouraged me to do the same. I did my best to follow his path of travel through the cold Colorado creek, but my older 1977 Yamaha DT400 MX Enduro, without the newer higher suspension, submerged into the creek, flooding out and stalling the engine. I jumped off as quick as I could and pushed the bike out of the water. Now the fun began.

After taking the spark plugs out of the motorcycle, we turned it upside down. I spent the next two and a half hours hand-cranking the kick starter, trying to pump all the water we could out of the motorcycle's engine.

As the afternoon turned into evening, I asked my guide how much longer we had to ride and if he thought it would be ok to ride it after dark.

"Well, I certainly did not intend to ride this last part of the trail in the dark, but I think we can make it."

It wasn't the inspirational "we can do it" speech I was looking for, but it was the truth.

After what seemed like forever, I finally got the old bike to fire over and got it started. Off we went, sticking close together on the trail, staying focused on the path right in front of us. With darkness all around and unsure terrain on the downhill side of the trail, I did my best to keep my nerve and stay calm, thankful for my bright headlight.

Finally, after about an hour of up-hill, white-knuckle riding, we emerged out of the wooded trail, onto the gravel road and made our way back to camp.

As we undressed from our riding gear and settled around the fire to talk about our awesome adventure, I asked my guide about the dark downhill areas we rode through. He said those areas were two-, and at times, up to three-thousand-foot ravines...some serious drop-offs merely inches from the narrow trail. Those were the areas he was talking about earlier when he said he didn't want to ride those areas in the dark.

Needless to say, I am glad we both made it through safely and lived to tell about it!

Sharing these outstanding experiences together with Debbie was so much fun, an amazing life adventure, that helped build the foundation for our relationship.

Debbie

As the warm summer sun turned cool, my days were filled with volleyball practices and games, along with sophomore level classes at Carl Sandburg. Volleyball was my favorite. The strategy, skills, teamwork and timing required to win games was a thrill for me as a setter and outside hitter.

Our Lady Chargers team gelled together throughout the season, winning most of our matches, landing us a spot in the post-season tournament in northern IL.

With my biggest cheerleader in the stands, yelling and whistling in support, we played well against teams with much larger enrollment than ours, but lost just before the finals.

I learned valuable life lessons from my coaches and teammates during those two years. Our motto and team chant still ringing in my ears… "P.M.A. all the way!" Positive Mental Attitude was drilled into us by our coaches, further developing my foundation that would prove to serve me well throughout my lifetime.

With a few short days of rest, I jumped right into a hectic basketball schedule. A transfer student joined our team from our rival school just an hour away. An excellent post player, Anna led the nation in rebounds and field goal percentage. Anna and I quickly became friends, and we set a goal for our team to beat our rival on our home court and earn a spot in the National tournament for the second year in a row.

In an exciting, high scoring game, we conquered our first goal by defeating our rival in front of our enthusiastic home crowd! Oh, that was sweet!

Enjoying the thrill of victory was short-lived as we endured the agony of defeat in the finals, eliminating us from another trip to Nationals. Extremely disappointed, that was a hard loss to get over.

I've always been a player to take the blame for a loss, setting the bar so high, thinking I could have played better. Like I let my coaches and teammates down. Losing was hard. And so was learning to be a gracious loser. More real-life lessons that helped shape who I am today.

Anna and I were recruited to play Division I basketball at the University of Evansville (UE) in Indiana, with full-ride basketball scholarships…an opportunity of a lifetime! We both accepted and made plans to transition our lives to Indiana in August.

Before my sophomore year ended, Tim moved back to Mississippi, this time to Vicksburg, in search of a better job opportunity.

Struggling with being several states apart again, Tim and I agreed that I would move to Vicksburg for the summer, so we could have those two and a half months together, before I headed to Evansville to start my junior year. If I had only known what life-changing decision lay just around the corner.

2

The Summer That Changed Everything

June 1986

Debbie

Just a few months before moving, I borrowed $1000 from the wedding fund my parents were saving for me, to buy a black Ford Torino, with low miles, from a little old lady...seriously.

So I packed up my belongings that hot, summer day, armed with my folded up map, lunch in the cooler, and a vision of being held in my fiancé's strong arms. I began the 12-hour trek from my hometown to unknown territory, by myself, with no air conditioning. Did I mention that it was a black car, with black interior, and a humid, sunny day?

About halfway through my trip, driving south on I-55 in Missouri, the sun-scorched pavement chewed up the tired, worn threads of one of my tires, forcing me to pull over and change my tire. Thankfully, I had a spare. And thankfully, my dad taught me how to change a tire. Thanks, Dad!

OK, problem solved and back on the road. Just one hour

from my destination, another tire blew. Remember, I bought this car from a little old lady. My dry-rotted tires were no match for the flaming Mississippi roadways. By this time, I was tired, hot, hungry, frustrated…and did not have another spare.

I walked to the nearest exit in the blistering heat and made it to the gas station to call Tim (no cell phones back then). An hour later, I fell into the arms of my Knight in Shining Armor, crying in frustration, yet thankful to be rescued.

What a great start to our fairy tale summer!

I quickly found a job, and we enjoyed spending our evenings and weekends together, playing softball, shooting hoops and hanging out.

With no accountability, and being away from the structure of family, friends, and church, we gave in to the temptations we allowed ourselves to face, and our physical relationship went to a level we were not prepared for.

Tim

We tried to keep our word to one another to stop at the boundary we had set for ourselves, but that proved to be very difficult. The truth is, we became very comfortable with our relationship and took risks that we now know have long term consequences.

About a month later, Debbie told me she was late for her period. Needless to say, I was not prepared to hear those words, but I tried to be brave and reasonable. I reassured her it would be ok and to wait a few days before getting a pregnancy test.

Debbie

Several days passed. Fear gripped me. *I can't be pregnant!*
My stomach in knots, Tim and I sat in the clinic waiting

room, anxious to receive the pregnancy test results. I silently pleaded with God for a negative result.

Moments later, we heard those fateful words, "Congratulations, you're pregnant!"

I was shocked.

Fear consumed me as we made our way to the truck.

As soon as Tim shut the door, the truth set in. I burst into tears, crying uncontrollably.

We were being so careful.

How could I have let this happen?

Why did we put ourselves in this position?

Why wasn't I stronger to stay true to my convictions?

What will our parents think?

Our families.

They will be so disappointed and hurt.

I've let them down.

I've compromised my values and faith for a few moments of pleasure.

Tim tried to console me, but there was nothing he could do to change our present reality.

Over the next few days, these questions and fears created a fog, robbing me of clarity and peace. With my start date at UE just weeks away, the pressure mounted.

We had no idea where to turn for help. Tim confided in someone we trusted (the only person we told), who mentioned abortion.

I had very little understanding of the biology of my body and pregnancy, and no idea what an abortion was. But this sounded like our only way out.

I told myself, *This is our only option. No one will have to know of our failure. No one will be hurt or disappointed in us. We won't be embarrassed. Everything will go back to normal, and I won't lose my scholarship, education or reputation.*

Believing these lies, and looking for an easy way out, we set the appointment…a decision that would forever change the course of our lives.

Tim

I remember just wanting to turn back the clock. To go back to the moment where I had the opportunity to honor Debbie and truly show her my love by keeping our commitment.

But that time had passed and now all I could think about was keeping our secret. Because of our upbringing, we both were carrying a very heavy load of guilt and shame. In our pain, we made a terrible decision to cover our sin…to get an abortion.

When the fateful day came, I drove her to Jackson, Mississippi, for the appointment. Honestly, I don't remember all the details, and I thank God for that, because what He allowed me to remember is painful enough.

I remember it was very hot outside, as you can imagine a Mississippi summer day would be. The hour drive to Jackson seemed to take three hours, as we sat in silence, me holding Debbie's hand, trying to comfort, support and reassure her in any way I could.

We finally reached the hospital where the abortion would be performed and I remember feeling a little at ease because it was a hospital. I knew doctors and nurses had to take an oath to "do no harm."

Should be safe, right?
They will help us.
They will help Debbie.
These guys are the professionals.
It's all going to be ok.

This line of thinking helped me relax.

I tried to show courage. I didn't want Debbie to see fear in me, so I did the best I could to help her feel relaxed and confident in the hospital and the staff.

We signed in and sat down to wait our turn. It wasn't long until the nurse came to get her. Debbie got up and walked away like she had no fear. I just sat in silence, alone in my chair, praying that God would someday forgive me. That someday He would allow Debbie to forgive me as well.

I remember feeling broken and useless, the enemy beating me down with my guilt and shame. I prayed for the doctor to be kind to Debbie and to be at his best at that moment with what he was about to do.

I desperately prayed over and over again, *Father, please don't let her be hurt anymore. I have brought her too much pain already. Father, please don't let her be hurt anymore.*

Before I knew it, the nurse was wheeling Debbie out in a wheelchair. The cover up for the summer of fun was done.

I don't remember much talking on the way home. I just tried to hold her and comfort her like before, but I knew she was hurting in every way.

Debbie

I remember the torturous ride back to Vicksburg, every tiny bump we hit escalating the severe cramping and pain in my abdomen. The bleeding and pain continued for several days, forcing me to stay in bed and miss work.

I remember the kids of some friends of ours, asking what was wrong with me. Tim told them I was sick and would be better in a few days. The first lie as a result of our decision.

A week later, the pain subsided, but the bleeding did not. It was time for me to head back to Illinois to see my family, pack for college, and get the required sports physical exam from my doctor.

With my bags loaded, Tim and I stood beside my car, holding each other tightly, not wanting to let go. Not wanting to be separated again. Not wanting to face my family.

With tears streaming down our cheeks, and one final kiss, we said goodbye, hoping we could leave this behind us, like nothing ever happened.

During the long, lonely drive home to Illinois, dread crept in, as every mile took me closer to the reunion with my family. Not being a good liar, I feared my secret would be written all over my face.

Pulling in our driveway, I buried my emotions, said a prayer, and greeted my family with a smile on my face. We hugged and chatted about my trip, as I steered clear of any details of what happened the past two weeks.

At the doctor's office a few days later, I remember sitting in the small room, waiting for my physical exam. My mom was a nurse there, so I was terrified they would somehow know what happened.

After my urine sample, the lab tech (a friend from our church) told me and my mom there was blood in my urine and asked if I had just finished my period.

I said, "Yes."

Lie #2.

I remember immediately feeling crushed for lying to her and my mom. But, I was relieved that they didn't run a pregnancy test. *Whew. Dodged that bullet.*

I couldn't wait to get to Evansville. To start my life over. To hide away from my family, my hometown and the fears that held me captive.

There was a problem though. I was still bleeding. Some bleeding after abortion is normal, but this was not normal. I remember finding a phone on campus, somewhere discreet, and calling the hospital where I had the abortion. The nurse sounded concerned and said I could have an ectopic pregnancy.

"What is that?" I stammered.

She explained that the embryo may have attached outside of the uterus where the baby is unable to survive and would cause dire complications for me. Fear again consumed me.

"You mean I could still be pregnant? And could have to have another surgery?"

"Yes," she answered.

Here I was, all alone, in a new city, knowing only one person - my best friend - who I definitely could not tell.

I called Tim crying hysterically. He calmed me down and encouraged me to follow the nurse's instructions and wait to see what happens. Desperate to hide my red, swollen eyes (and my secret) from my roommate, I found a private place to process this scary information.

By the grace of God, the bleeding stopped. Thankfully, I did not have an ectopic pregnancy. To say I was relieved is a gross understatement. I finally felt like my secret was safe from anyone finding out. While that weight was lifted, the burden of guilt and shame quickly took its place.

Tim

Receiving that frantic phone call tore me up inside. The reality that I wasn't there for Debbie smacked me in the face. I remember praying for God to heal her. Thank God she got better physically and recovered with great health.

Now the true test began, as to how we would carry this secret as we pursued a life together.

How would we carry the burden of what we had done, as we tried to

grow spiritually and to build relationships with others?
How would we re-build trust between us?

Because I love her, I was hurting as well. With our hearts broken and committed to keep our secret, we put on our happy masks and tried our best to move forward with our life and relationship.

3

Life Goes On

Debbie

Pretending like nothing happened, the excitement and busyness of campus life at UE quickly overtook any feelings of regret as I threw myself into classes, homework, and practices.

Through the ectopic scare, Tim and I realized how much we needed each other's support as the long-distance situation just wasn't working. He packed his bags and headed for Indiana, trusting to find work and a place to live when he arrived.

Tim

I got to Evansville with about $200 to my name. I rented a one room apartment for $25 a week. It was upstairs and I had to share a bathroom in the hallway with the guy in the next apartment. My room had a bed, a table, a kitchenette, a chair, a lamp stand, a dresser and a small black and white TV.

I can do this. I can make it. God please help me.

It wasn't long before I found a job at a factory, painting the inside of computer parts. I worked 3rd shift and actually liked it. I would go into work at 11pm, clock out at 7am, go home and sleep till 1pm. Then I'd go see Debbie and play pick-up basketball at the gym where the girls held their practice.

Even though I was not a student on campus, everyone was used to seeing me around.

I didn't make a lot of money, but it kept the bills paid and a little food in the cupboards. Let's just put it this way: I ate a lot of crackers and milk…and I would do it all again!

It is amazing what you will do for someone you love. Someone you know is your life mate. Someone you share something with that no one else on the planet shares or knows.

Debbie

Through connections with my hometown church, we found a small, loving community of believers in Evansville who helped us grow relationally and spiritually. We particularly enjoyed attending a home Bible study, developing strong friendships with mature believers.

Living on campus offered more accountability regarding our relationship, as I felt responsible to my roommate and teammates. There were a few occasions however, when our desire to have quality time together led to a few overnights at Tim's apartment. Sadly, the lure of pleasure was stronger than our convictions and the fear of another pregnancy. The guilt was crippling.

We knew we were meant to spend the rest of our lives together. We wanted to get married, but having spent my wedding fund on the Torino, the lack of money held us back.

I remember sitting on the bus during a road trip with my basketball team, sharing my struggles with my best friend, Anna. I never was one to really pour my heart out, but to share just enough of what I thought people needed to know. I now see that was a way to keep others somewhat at a distance. I had a secret to protect. I couldn't let people into my life too deeply or they might find out.

A few days after that conversation, Anna told me a friend of hers wanted to give us $1500 so we could get married! $1500! That was a lot of money to a poor college student and a 21-year-old factory worker. I couldn't fathom why God would bless us in this way after what we had done. The unworthiness crept in.

We graciously accepted the offer and began planning our June wedding. Actually, my mom took care of most of the details, as the wedding would be in our hometown, six hours away. Thanks again, Mom!

Remember, I'm still a tomboy at heart, so a big, frilly wedding was not appealing to me. I just wanted to keep it simple (and cheap!). My sister, Cindy, had just gotten married in November, and we were about the same size, so I bought her dress for $125.

Our church didn't have air conditioning at the time, so we rented another church for the ceremony, then held the reception in the basement of our church where it was cooler. Remember those paper bells and streamers? Yep, that was the extent of our decorations!

For refreshments, we planned to have punch, nuts, my mom's homemade rose mints, and a beautiful cake (with the plastic bride and groom on top, of course).

That's what you do when you are on a shoe-string budget!

The big day finally came - June 13, 1987.

The sun shone brightly on that beautiful Saturday afternoon, as our family and friends filled the church sanctuary.

Tim's dad and my pastor led the ceremony, following the traditional order and reading First Corinthians 13, the well-known love chapter.

When it was time to exchange rings, Tim's hands were swollen due to the heat, making it a challenge to get his ring on his finger! I was thankful for the chuckle we shared, which helped me relax a bit.

With sweat rolling down his face, we both said, "I do," sealing our covenant with God and each other, in front of many witnesses.

To everyone's surprise, after the kiss, one of Tim's older nephews shouted, "Praise the Lord!" Makes me smile just thinking about it.

Looking at our wedding pictures now is hilarious, with both of us sporting our fashionable, loose curl mullets and a nervous smile plastered on my face!

You'll never guess where we went for our honeymoon…Six Flags! We both only had a few days off work, so before we headed back to Evansville, we spent that Monday riding roller coasters. My favorite was the Screaming Eagle. I don't know what happened, because now, I hate roller coasters!

We were happy newlyweds, ready to finally develop our relationship without guilt, and to put our past behind us. This was our time to start over. To begin our lives together as one.

Tim

Now married, this was a very happy time, as we were feeling like our plan to keep moving forward with the American dream was working. Life was good.

Still not talking about our past, we enjoyed our little modest life, thankful to the Lord for His grace and mercy. We didn't know what our future would hold, but we believed that together, Debbie and I could face any challenge and make it through.

By this time, I had a better job. With her scholarship covering our rent, we leased an upstairs apartment close to campus, and were doing ok.

Debbie's coach was not my biggest fan, thinking our getting married would distract his star player. But, little did he know how great she would be.

As her senior season began, and wins started racking up, many media interviews and newspaper articles highlighted their success. I was Debbie's biggest cheerleader, attending every home and away game that I could, encouraging her to "Shoot the ball!"

I truly believe if she would have shot every time I yelled at her to shoot, she would have averaged 30 points a game instead of 19!

The team finished the season with 21 wins and 7 losses, improving their previous year's record of 19-9, and emerged as Midwest Collegiate Conference (MCC) champions!

As the leading scorer, Debbie finished the season with 532 points (most in school history at the time), setting a new UE record for made shots (225). She was honored as the MCC Player of the Year (only player in program history at that time to earn this honor), UE Female Athlete of the Year (first basketball player to earn this award), Academic All-American (first player in UE history), and graduated with a Bachelor's of Science degree, Cum Laude.

God truly blessed her, while her true nature was being revealed as the leader she was, and the leader she would become.

I believe it to be so important to let people know about all the accolades Debbie received. Even after our grievous sin and cover up, God the Father showed us love and compassion. He lavished us with rewards and heaped praise on us. Not to show

Debbie's greatness, but to reveal our Father's greatness.

He so beautifully showed us His love in a way that meant the most to us, as our entire life had been in sports. To receive the highest honor in her field was a loud and clear message for me that God was for us and not against us.

Debbie

Balancing school, basketball, church activities, friendships and marriage brought challenges, but I thrived on staying busy. The busier the better…that way I didn't have to think about the dark secret lurking deep in my heart.

Not once, in the two years since the abortion, did Tim and I talk about it. That whole experience was stuffed. Buried. Never to be resurrected, as far as I was concerned. Or so I hoped.

4

New Beginnings

Debbie

The day after I graduated, early May 1988, Tim and I packed our meager belongings and moved to a rental home in Springfield, Illinois, to work with his brother and be closer to family. I landed an entry-level assistant position at a corporate fitness center and enjoyed teaching aerobics (think Jane Fonda!) and helping individuals reach their fitness goals. We attended a church with Tim's brother and family, settling into our new life.

While our lives looked pretty normal on the outside, I struggled with trust issues. I had trusted Tim that what we were doing intimately before we were married was not crossing the line. And I trusted him to protect me.

Now, that trust was broken. The foundation of trust that strong relationships are built upon was fractured before we even said, "I do."

I was skeptical of Tim and his faithfulness to me, always having this nagging little voice whispering in my ear that I couldn't trust him. Obviously, this created arguments and further damage to our relationship.

We bought our first house the summer of 1989, and discovered we were pregnant shortly after.

Now, the words, "Congratulations, you're pregnant!" brought exuberant joy and excitement! We eagerly shared our news with family and friends. Now, I could be a Mom, a desire I longed to embrace, in hopes to fill the ache in my empty arms.

Just a few shorts weeks later, I started bleeding, then cramping. Terrified, I called my doctor, who informed me that I may be miscarrying…words no mother wants to hear.

I stayed home and rested as my body released my tiny baby from my womb. I remember how emotionally drained and exhausted I was following the miscarriage. Expressing this to my doctor, he dismissed my concerns by minimizing the amount of blood I had lost. No compassion. No encouragement. Another blow to my fragile spirit.

The flood of haunting memories that I had stuffed so far down, came rushing to the surface, along with a torrent of shame-filled thoughts.

I didn't realize it at the time, but it was the enemy pummeling me with lies:

I took the life of my child, so God is mad at me.
This is the punishment I deserve.
I'm not worthy to be a Mom.
I will never have another baby.

Sadly, the lies wove themselves into the fabric of my being, as I embraced them as truth, further damaging my already broken heart.

Tim

After our move to Illinois, I was helping manage a pawn shop and hustling to make a living for my new wife. Debbie was working and seemed to be doing ok. She seemed healthy and content.

We never talked about the abortion, and I truly believe that trauma was the root of our struggles as a young married couple. We looked good on the outside, but she was struggling to trust me again and I knew it. The message was sometimes more loud and clear than others.

I am thankful for the wonderful role model in my father. I grew up always seeing him take care of my mother. Always working and doing whatever needed to be done to give her a good, yet modest life. Even with our struggles, I always embraced my responsibility to provide for her, for us.

I was trying to settle into the American dream. You know…the wife, the house, 2.3 kids and the white picket fence. I desperately hoped it would be enough to someday win back her trust.

When Debbie got pregnant, of course, I was a very proud father. Things were so much different now. We both embraced the privilege and opportunity to be parents. Things still weren't great, but we were working through all the new compromises that we needed to make, necessary to live everyday with someone. I had to learn to go with the ebb and flow of our relationship.

When we miscarried, the wave came crashing down and it beat us up pretty good. I was heartbroken, not only because I had lost a child, but because my wife was hurting so badly.

We were miserable. The enemy tried his best to destroy us and kill our future together, but God had a different plan. We rallied around each other and like good soldiers, we did our best to keep marching on.

Debbie

That November 1989, Galesburg High School developed

a Hall of Fame to honor past athletes, coaches, and teams for their accomplishments throughout school history. Incredibly, I was chosen as one of the Inaugural members! Having graduated only five years prior, this was quite an honor to be recognized amidst the decades of amazing talent that had walked the halls of our school.

At the induction ceremony, I remember someone asking me if I had any children yet. Answering a timid "No," a flash of shame surfaced, reminding me that I have had two children, but no baby in my arms. The lies crept in. *Do I really deserve this honor after what I've done? If they only knew, they would strip this award from me.*

Several days after the ceremony, I realized my period was late, so I took a pregnancy test and it showed positive! The flood of emotion and doubts poured in. *Really? I'm pregnant? God is giving me another chance to be a mom?*

It truly was hard to believe that God would be so gracious.

Fearing another miscarriage (after all, I believed I didn't deserve a baby), we waited until the first trimester had passed, then excitedly shared our wonderful news! I'm going to be a mom! (I now know that I was already a mother of two, but the enemy hid that truth from me, making me believe I robbed myself of that honor.)

I enjoyed an easy pregnancy, and endured a hot summer, in anticipation of our precious gift arriving August 10. Two weeks early, I went into labor.

Struggling for hours with major contractions, which dilated me to 7cm, my body would not progress. I was stuck at 7cm, yet the waves of pain escalated.

Finally, Tim couldn't stand to see me suffer any longer and agreed to the C-section the doctor recommended.

At 7:23pm, July 27, 1990, our precious baby boy was

delivered into this world. Francis Christian Shultz, named after his proud daddy.

Finally…I'm a mother. I have a baby. Thank you, God, for blessing us, even though we are unworthy.

Holding Christian in my arms filled my aching heart to the brim with happiness, joy, and gratitude. What a blessing from God! An undeserved blessing, but still a blessing.

As I grew weary after sleepless nights and adjusting to life with a newborn, the enemy again planted doubts and lies into my mind. Sadly, I believed the condemning words…*I don't deserve this baby. I'll never be a good mom.*

Suffering in silent pain, tears fell as the reality of those words cut deep into my heart, re-opening the already festering wound.

Tim

During the C-section, I was in the surgery room the entire time. I did not want to miss a single second of my baby coming into this world. With what I had done to my first baby, and miscarrying our second baby, I would not be moved.

Refusing to be left in the lobby alone again, I stayed by Debbie's side, as the doctors and nurses did their jobs, and delivered our beautiful, big-headed baby boy. A boy! I was beside myself with gratefulness to the Lord. Don't get me wrong, if this baby was a girl, I would have been just as happy.

But, I felt like God gave me something more. I believed in that moment He was showing me His unmerited love, through my newborn son, that my name would go on. In my spirit and in my being, I believe this was a victory over the enemy and I was deeply thankful for it.

By this time, I landed a new job at the Illinois Department of Transportation (IDOT) in the Motorcycle Safety Division.

I met a lot of great people there and built a close friendship with my co-worker, Tony. He was about 20 years my senior and I viewed him as a second father-figure. Tony was the kind of guy who would give me $100 for Christmas to bless my young family.

I was thankful for the steady income and the security of having full health insurance, especially with a new baby. Gratitude filled my heart as I recognized God's goodness by giving me another chance to be a father. And my wife was a new person. She seemed so happy.

5

Blessings in the Midst of the Storm

Debbie

Just before Christmas, 1990, a job opportunity opened to work with parents and pre-schoolers in their home, teaching parents how to use everyday household items to interact and teach their children. With teaching being one of my giftings, I jumped at the chance to invest into families in this way.

Less than a year later, I discovered I was pregnant, and was overjoyed to receive another blessing from God! Our beautiful baby girl, Kasey Lee, was born March 15, 1992, with no complications, thankfully.

God had been tugging on my heart to resign from my job and stay home with our children, trusting Him to provide financially for our family. Taking a giant leap of faith, Tim agreed. As my short maternity leave ended, I agreed to complete the current school year in May, then resign for the next session.

What an amazing blessing to not have to get myself and two kids ready every morning, work all day, fix supper, baths, clean house, grocery shop, church activities, teach aerobics at my side job….and be a wife! Many women do all of this, and more. I honestly don't know how they juggle everything. It was too much for me.

My heart melted as I cuddled my newborn and almost two-year old, reading books, going on walks and to our favorite parks. The slow pace allowed me to finally breathe, to be still and in the moment.

However, I soon realized that being still is not the best scenario for someone hiding pain. Going from 100 miles an hour every day, to no structure, and no apparent "purpose," brought a mild depression, which began to cloud my mind and spirit, robbing me of my inner peace. In the stillness, the voices returned, stripping away my confidence and my identity in Christ. The doubts swirled, and the pain re-surfaced, further deteriorating my trust in Tim and in God.

I'm an inward processor. I would take things in, piles of rubbish in my mind and spirit, until I would explode like a volcano. And guess who felt the brunt of this backlash? My husband and my kids. Never did I expose myself to those outside my home, though. I had to keep up my facade, my happy-face mask, so everyone would think that our lives were good. No problems here.

So often, I would be angry about something completely unrelated to Tim, but would misplace my anger toward him, creating confusion and misunderstandings in our relationship.

Fear also gripped my heart…fear of losing Tim to someone else, fear of not having enough money, fear that Tim's relationship with God was not what I thought it should be.

As Tim spiritually straddled the fence, I took on the role as the head of the household. Carrying the burden for Tim's salvation, I found myself nagging at him about this and that, challenging him to step up and make better decisions. I believed I could change him to be what I thought a Christian husband and father should look like.

That didn't work.

Ultimately, my actions pushed Tim farther away from me and farther away from God. Our marriage was crumbling, and I didn't know how to fix it. We were basically co-existing in the same household, with minimal meaningful conversations or kisses or touches... happiness and joy faded away.

Several years passed as we trudged along in life, broken and weary, not realizing that the root cause of our troubles was buried deep in our hearts.

Tim

When our beautiful baby Kasey was born, my heart was overflowing with love and pride. The kids were only nineteen months apart, so needless to say, we were busy. But I thought life was good.

Together, we decided we didn't want someone else to raise our kids, so Debbie quit her job and became a stay at home mom. The toughest job in the world, I might add. But, we both knew it was the best decision for our family in that season of our life.

Things seemed to be going along as good as they could, for a young, one-income family. I was working full time and making a humble wage. Debbie was a wizard with our finances, always keeping the bills paid, in spite of my lack of self-control with our debit card.

When she felt like she wasn't being productive, I would remind her that being a homemaker and stay-at-home mom is a hard job, and the most important job anyone could have.

Little did I know she was not mad or upset with me so

much, but the evil one was bombarding her mind with negative thoughts again and she was being tormented by it. When she unleashed on me, I just tried to bury myself in work, playing ball and taking care of my kids, the best way I knew how. I always tried to show them love and do my best to have time with them, trying to give Debbie the space she seemed to need.

After a few years of living like roommates and sharing parenting duties, I'd had it with everything and everybody. It seemed like nothing I did was ever good enough, or at least not good enough for Debbie. Things were not good, but we were committed to stay together, having made a covenant with God.

Debbie

Throughout our early relationship, I believed we would have three children, so I felt our family was incomplete. But, with the struggles we were experiencing, I didn't see how we could have any more children.

By the grace of God, I got pregnant in the summer of 1995. While our relationship was not healthy, we happily welcomed the news, thankful to grow our family.

Tim

When Debbie told me she was pregnant, I was shocked, but thankful. We headed to the hospital on April Fool's Day, as Debbie's labor started. I remember thinking, *OK, God is going to give me another boy because this is opening day for baseball!*

Debbie and I watched the Cubs on TV, as she progressed through labor. My friends, let me tell you, God has a sense of humor! I was all ready for a boy, and out came this beautiful little baby girl, our precious Kendall Marie!

My heart was smitten again. God knew she was just what I needed to get myself together. To start doing a better job of loving my wife like Christ loves the church. This new bundle of joy God had blessed us with was my inspiration.

Even though I had a renewed sense of responsibility for my wife and young family, I was done with main stream religion and the traditions of men. I stopped going to church with Debbie and the kids, even though it caused problems between her and I. It didn't matter.

I had been around church my whole life and was tired of the indifference in the church. I was fed up with the religious spirit that seemed to control so many houses of worship. Needing renewal of some kind, I was looking everywhere, even in the wrong places. Even though I was floundering, I never wanted to be without my family. I always kept believing that if we could just stay together, we would be alright.

Debbie

Taking the kids to church by myself was not pleasant. It was embarrassing for me, mainly because our cover was blown. Everything was not ok in our home, and now everyone knew it. Even though Tim was willing to try other churches, I struggled with the idea. Having attended our church for eight years, we had many friendships and were actively involved on many committees, served as VBS director for several years, and helped with the youth group. I feared what people would say or think about us. Plus, I didn't trust Tim to lead our family, so I doubted his decision to go elsewhere.

That December, God spoke into my heart that it was more important to submit to my husband than to fear people and their opinions. With a trembling step of faith, I resigned from my positions and agreed to visit other churches as a family. That was one of the hardest decisions I had made to that point, but I now see it was one of the best decisions we made in our lives.

As we visited churches, I began seeking God about Tim's relationship with Him in a new way. One day, as I was praying for him, God spoke very directly into my spirit, saying, *You are not the Holy Spirit. I want you to love him and pray for him.*

Talk about a wake-up call! The scales fell from my eyes and I realized that I had been trying to do God's job all these years. I was actually getting in God's way.

I prayed for forgiveness for taking on a responsibility that I had not been given and asked for His help to love Tim well and to sincerely pray for him. I finally surrendered Tim into God's hands and trusted Him to do what only He can do…rescue him. I felt a shift in my spirit…like a load lifted off me. Yes, this was God.

I prayed for Tim with a pure heart, that God's love would fill him and transform his heart. And I started to show him love in ways I hadn't done in years. Little things. At first, I didn't see any impact and would get discouraged. And I definitely didn't do this perfectly, but I would humble myself and ask for forgiveness when I failed. I believe God used my humility to soften Tim's heart. And then Tony died.

II.

Transformation

6

Turning Point

March 1997

Tim

For seven years, I worked at the Illinois Department of Transportation, leading the Motorcycle Safety program alongside Tony. He never claimed to have a relationship with Jesus and I was living in rebellion, so the topic of salvation and Jesus never came up in our relationship.

Because of my personal pain, which caused me to have a bad attitude, I became negligent in my role as a husband and father regarding spiritual things, where it really matters.

Tony knew how I was living my life at the time. I was running with the devil through the week and taking my wife and kids to church on Sundays. I never dealt with anything of substance that was going on in my life. But, I knew I couldn't keep living the way I was. I needed a wake-up call.

On March 8, I went to work like a normal day. When I arrived, I realized Tony wasn't at work, so I checked the big board to see if he was scheduled to be out of town working. To my surprise he was not on the board and no one had heard from him yet that morning. I remember going back to my office and didn't really think about it again. I knew if he needed anything or if he was in trouble he would contact me.

It wasn't long until our direct supervisor came in my office and sat down. I knew something was up because his eyes were red, like he'd been crying. He told me Tony had passed away the night before from a massive stroke. I was instantly heartbroken and began to weep uncontrollably. As I struggled to keep my emotions together, I asked my supervisor if I could go out to my car for a few minutes. I needed a moment to grieve in private and get my emotions under control.

I escaped down the stairs so no one would see me on the elevator. I ran out of the building to my car and just sat there alone in the cold, crying like a little child. I loved Tony and not knowing for sure if he had a relationship with Jesus was breaking my heart.

As I sat there in the quiet, weeping, I realized I had never taken the time to share with Tony what I believe about Jesus as the Son of God, the Savior of the world. That no matter what, Jesus loved him. That Romans 10:9 says, *"If you declare with your mouth, 'Jesus is Lord,' and believe in your heart that God raised him from the dead, you will be saved."*

In my world growing up in the church, older Christian people passed away and I didn't think anything about it. I just assumed they died and went to heaven. I was also taught that if someone passed away without accepting the gift of salvation from Jesus, they were eternally separated from God and His Son, Jesus.

That day in the car and for a week or so after, I was an emotional basket case. I cried every day, begging God to forgive me for not extending His love to Tony. I told the Lord, *If You will just give me another chance, I will do better. I will be a better husband. I will be a better father, a better friend, a better servant. I will work on my relationship with You and do my best to work out my salvation daily.*

Needless to say, this event impacted our family in a big way. But, what the devil meant for harm, God turned into something beautiful! I got out the Bible my wife had bought for me years before and started reading again. It was amazing how the Word of God seemed to come alive to me! The realization of His forgiveness was overwhelming, and the desire to please my heavenly Father consumed me.

As I followed the Lord's leading to stay in His Word and to get His Word into my spirit, He led me to this scripture in Ephesians 5:13-17,

> "But everything exposed by the light becomes visible, for it is light that makes everything visible. This is why it is said: 'Wake up, O sleeper, rise from the dead, and Christ will shine on you.' Be very careful, then, how you live — not as unwise but as wise, making the most of every opportunity, because the days are evil. Therefore, do not be foolish, but understand what the Lord's will is."

Wow! I honestly believe, in that moment that night at my dining room table, my life truly turned around. I was so thankful to God for another chance to spread His love to others. I was truly awakened!

My new come-to-Jesus moment was a great relief to Debbie. Everything she had been praying for was coming to pass!

This was the start of the restoration of our relationship and marriage. Through all the struggles, we stayed together. God helped us to never give up, to always keep fighting. I believe the competitive spirit He put in both of us, helped us recover and realize with God all things were possible. Even forgiveness and redemption for us, for the grievous sin we committed. Thank you, Jesus for your forgiveness!

Armed with my newfound freedom, I was ready for something more. I knew I couldn't settle for less than what I believed God had for me, so I started searching.

After work one day I was sitting in my easy chair, catching up with the kids and asking about their day at school. The television was on and I was surfing the channels. When I stopped on our local cable channel, there was an ad from a new pastor and his church. I remember him saying, "If you're looking for a church that is alive, come and give us a try!" I vividly remember the Lord prompting me that this was our new church and that I needed to go over and see the pastor right then!

I first thought, *Tim, this is crazy.* Then I remembered what I promised God, that when He speaks to me, I would do my best to always say, "Yes, Lord." So, I shouted up the stairs to Debbie, where she was doing laundry, that I had just seen an advertisement for a new church and I believed that God wanted me to go over right now and talk to the pastor.

I hopped in the car and drove over to the church, which was only five minutes from our house. Excited to see what God had in store for me, I pulled into the parking lot, only to find the church was closed for the day. I sat in my car facing the building and I began to pray something like this, *Lord, thank you for this church. Thank you for this pastor and this opportunity. Please Lord, let this be the church. Let this be the pastor and the people you have prepared for my family to be a part of. Lord, please let this be real…because if it's not, I don't ever want to be a part of church again.*

The next Sunday, Debbie and I loaded up the kids and went to visit this church, believing for the best. The lead pastor was out of town, so his senior associate was preaching. I vividly remember his sincere kindness, which helped us feel safe and right at home. As Debbie and I walked out after service, holding hands, we both knew in our spirit that this was the right church. This was the group of people He wanted us to grow with for the next season of our lives.

Debbie

All my life, my beliefs and understanding kept God in a box. A small box, that I thought He fit in. I prayed for people, because that's what a Christian is supposed to do, but I didn't really believe that God would answer my prayers.

As we faithfully attended our new church, I started to realize how big God really is, and that He does answer prayer! I saw that firsthand in the transformation in my husband!

Seeing God moving so mightily in Tim created a desire within me for more of God...a spiritual hunger that the world could not satisfy. My relationship with Him seemed shallow, with roots, but not very deep ones. I needed and wanted Him more than ever before.

As I sought God, He met me right where I was in my brokenness and weakness. I let Him love me like never before. I embraced His forgiveness in a new way, and I grew closer to Him. Tim did as well.

As we both focused on God, rather than each other, putting Him first and keeping our eyes on Him, we not only drew closer to God, but to each other!

You may have heard it explained like this: Draw a triangle, and write God at the top, then yourself and your spouse at each bottom corner. Draw arrows from the bottom corners up toward God. As you both grow closer to God, you will naturally grow closer to each other.

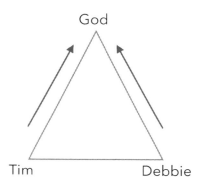

God

Tim   Debbie

Supernaturally, God began healing our marriage, putting the shattered pieces back together, one piece at a time.

In July, a special speaker came to our church for revival services. At the end of one of the services, he started prophesying and speaking words of affirmation over people in the congregation. I was not at all familiar with this spiritual gift, so I was a little freaked out. And then he picked me out of the crowd.

Me? There are hundreds of people here...why me? I questioned.

He asked me to walk forward toward the altar.

Everything inside of me objected, wanting to stay in my seat, safely by my husband's side. But, I submitted, although afraid, and walked toward him.

He said that he saw me pregnant, and not a spiritual pregnancy, but a natural pregnancy. He said I would give birth to a son, and he would be a powerful preacher of the Word of God, leading many to Christ!

I couldn't believe what I was hearing...it was quite

overwhelming.

Remember, I always believed we would have three children, and our third child was just over a year old at this time. Tim and I never dreamed or discussed having more children. After getting over the shock, we talked to our pastor about it and he encouraged us to give it to the Lord, and if it was His will, it would happen.

We prayed about it, and left it at that, not really thinking about it much more. Tim and I both grew spiritually by leaps and bounds, as God's love filled each of our hearts, showing us how to forgive and love each other well.

Tim

With the Lord back at His rightful place in our lives and with Debbie and I seeking more of the Lord daily, our family was content and happy. Life was very good.

By this time, we were totally involved with our church and I was drawing closer than ever before to Jesus.

When Debbie got singled out to receive a word from God through the visiting evangelist, I remember selfishly thinking, *OK God. I'm sitting right here. Why did you pick her and not me?*

I was so hungry for the things of God, I wanted more.

As the Lord started speaking through this man, I was taken aback. Instantly I thought, *Lord, we already have three kids and only one income…what's going on?*

As I listened closely to my Father speaking through this man, declaring all the things my son would do for His kingdom, I remember being filled with boldness and thankfulness for His kindness.

We embraced this powerful word from the Lord and, if it was meant to be, we believed He would make it so.

Not long after this, He kindled a passion in me to travel to other countries, to love the unloved, to share kindness, gentleness and hope with those who the world overlooks. Again, I said yes, not knowing where He was taking me.

Debbie

A year later, 1998, Tim and I were preparing to travel on our first mission trip to Guatemala with a small group of people from our church. Let me just throw in here that God incredibly provided $2,400 for Tim and I to go minister together on this trip! Remember, we are living on one income, raising three children. We were in awe as He poured out His blessings through family and friends.

God simply demonstrated His extravagant love to us, His forgiven children, as we stepped out by faith and trusted Him to provide. He is so good!

We were scheduled to leave early August to share the good news of Jesus and hold medical clinics in remote villages near Antigua. Two weeks before we were to leave, I found out I was pregnant! What a shocker!

While surprised, we were excited when reminded of the words spoken over us 12 months ago (maybe to the day!).

I remember kneeling at the altar, asking God about this pregnancy, and if I should go on the trip.

He spoke so gently into my spirit, saying, *This pregnancy is a fulfillment of the prophecy. You will have a son and you are to name him David. Go on the trip. I will protect you.*

A peace and joy flooded my spirit, giving me such clarity and confidence that this was God's will!

My OB/GYN doctor was not so convinced. He advised us of the dangers associated with traveling in a third world country, emphasizing the deadly viruses mosquitos can transmit. But, armed with God's promise, I was determined to go on this trip.

After our plane landed in Guatemala City, we waited outside for our missionary to pick us up. The dense humidity settled on my skin, leaving a shimmer of sweat within minutes.

The next day, we literally hiked up the side of a mountain to a village where the indigenous people had never seen white people before, carrying our bedding and supplies on our backs. For a mother of three, I was in pretty good shape, so I enjoyed the physical challenge.

Sharing a testimony while having it translated, was the hardest part for me. Still timid, I preferred to stand in Tim's shadow, letting his fun personality shine. I struggled with what to say, thinking, *Lord, I really don't have any grand testimony to share. I've walked with You my whole life and you have been faithful.*

I seriously did not think about the abortion at that time, because I stuffed it so far down, and covered it up. I was growing in many other areas of my life, spiritually and relationally, that the abortion was out of sight, out of mind.

The food and water in a third world country can be harmful, even deadly. We were warned to never buy anything from a roadside stand.

When a plate of food prepared by the villagers was placed before us, we were instructed to accept it with gratitude and respect. Many times, they had just killed their last three chickens to feed our crew of 15, so we were expected to eat everything on our plate.

I ate what I could stomach, and not wanting to disrespect anyone, I encouraged Tim to finish the rest. He was gracious and thankfully agreed.

As several of our team were plagued with stomach issues and mosquito bites, God's grace carried me through, as He promised! One afternoon I had a minor stomach ache, after eating at a village where we strongly felt demonic oppression. After we left that evening, I was fine!

On our last day, we prepared to head back to the States, and were standing in the open-air courtyard of our beautiful hostel, with our luggage. All of a sudden, a mosquito bit me near my right wrist, the first one during the entire 10 days we were there. Imagine that…one mosquito bite after being in the mountains of Guatemala, exposed every moment of every day (and night). The bite got pretty big, about the size of a nickel.

At first, I was disappointed. *God, you said you would protect me.*

He gently responded, *This is to show you how easily you could have been bitten this entire trip, but I protected you.*

The bite quickly disappeared! What a great reminder not to take God's promises for granted, but to be humbly grateful for every promise kept.

Thankfully, we made it home safely, with no physical complications for my pregnancy, which I believe was a seed of faith planted into our doctor's heart.

When it was time for our first ultrasound, the sonographer asked if we thought we were having a boy or a girl. I confidently said, "It's a boy."

She asked how we knew, and we shared that God told us it was a boy. She said, "What if it's a girl?"

Again, I replied confidently, "Well, he will be a boy by the time he is born!" Ha!

I bet she thought we were crazy! But, that's how confident I was about the word God spoke to me that night I knelt at the altar.

She placed the transducer on my abdomen, and a grin spread across her face, as she said with a chuckle, "It's a boy." What a confirmation that I was hearing from the Lord!

About that same time, a week-long revival at our church

turned into a 9 month-long revival! The Spirit of God was pouring out, including signs, wonders, prophecies, healing and transformations! It was incredible to be saturated with God's presence, drawing me closer to Him. I believe David was also saturated as he basked in God's glory, tucked away in my womb.

With the travel bug intensifying after our first trip, Tim registered for the next Guatemala trip, February 18-28, 1999. Considering David wasn't due until March 28, he joined the team.

With his return flight scheduled for Sunday night, the 28th, I decided to take our three kids to Galesburg, to visit my parents for the weekend.

It was unseasonably warm that Saturday, so the kids broke their cabin fever by playing outside, running up and down the big hill at the park, and riding bikes.

Several hours later, I started having contractions! At first, I thought I could just rest, and maybe these were just false contractions. I had those early on with Kendall, so surely, that's what this was. Then I could drive home to see my doctor.

But, the contractions didn't stop...they got stronger. Fear gripped me. Here I am two hours away from home, and Tim is in Guatemala!!! At this point in our lives, he was my rock, and I didn't know how I would get through this without him.

Mom called the local hospital and they strongly encouraged me not to drive two hours to Springfield, with three children, by myself (thanks, Mom!), and to go to the ER immediately. I reluctantly submitted to their advice, and was admitted to the hospital, officially in labor.

My mom and sister did their best to fill Tim's shoes as my birthing partner. Several friends drove from Springfield to pray and support me. They even gave their best efforts to contact

Tim in Guatemala to let him know our son was soon to be born. Not that he could do anything about it! The team was scheduled to fly out the next day but wouldn't arrive in Springfield until late Sunday night.

Tim

I spent the week deep in the jungle serving the indigenous peoples, building housing and providing food, clothing and medical supplies. It was no cake walk. But the demanding physical labor made me feel alive!

As we came out of the jungle after seven days of no contact with the outside world, we returned to our hostel and settled in for our last night. My body ached from the hard work and rough nights wrestling with the air mattress. Exhausted, I slumped into bed. Within minutes, I was fast asleep.

It was about 11:30pm and I was awakened by someone shouting "Timoteo! Timoteo!" and that I had a phone call from home. As I ran to the front desk to get the call, my mind was racing with what was going on.

When I picked up the phone, the call dropped! The person who took the call could only tell me that my wife was in the hospital and because of the language barrier, that is all they could understand. I spent the rest of the night praying, snatching as much sleep as I could.

Debbie

As my labor progressed, I trusted that God was with me, and is my Rock. David (meaning "Beloved") Corban (meaning "Gift Devoted to God") entered this world early Sunday morning, February 28…exactly a month early!

He was small, 6 pounds, 5 ounces, but healthy and strong.

I was extremely grateful for God's grace and blessings, as He placed amazing family and friends in my life to pray me through.

Tim arrived at the hospital early Monday morning, disappointed that he wasn't there for me, but beaming with pride, as he held our newborn son. Our family of 6...now complete...reunited, full of love and thankfulness.

7

His Goodness Never Fails

Debbie

As a result of the move of God through the revival, along with the restoration of our marriage, my spiritual roots were growing deeper and I hungered for more of Him. Yet, I sensed a wall in my spirit that was hindering me from drawing nearer to Him.

I remember laying on the floor near the altar one Sunday evening service, and crying out to God, *What is the wall that is holding me back?*

Holy Spirit spoke so gently into my spirit, *You need to forgive yourself for the abortion.*

The abortion…that experience was buried and forgotten…by me, but not by God.

While I didn't realize I was still chained to my past, or that I was still holding myself accountable, He saw my spiritual bondage and wanted to set me free! The first step for me, after already confessing my sin and asking for forgiveness years before, was to forgive myself. To let myself off the hook.

I now know that holding onto sin, believing that my sin is worse than everyone else's, is actually pride.

That's like saying what Jesus did on the cross was not enough to cover my sin.

Forgiving myself was simply receiving and embracing what Jesus did through His death and resurrection as payment for my sin and trusting God's promise that my sin is gone as far as the east is from the west.

In that still, intimate moment, I prayed a simple prayer, *I forgive myself for the abortion.*

In that very moment, the wall in my spirit came crashing down, and I saw myself immediately cross over toward Jesus! What a massive breakthrough!

When I stood up, I felt different, and had the courage to walk over to one of the prayer leaders, Martha, and tell her what just happened. A wave of relief engulfed me, after surrendering my secret of 13 years!

As I walked up the aisle to my seat, Tim and I embraced as I shared my breakthrough, thankful for God's unfailing love. In that tender moment, Tim received freedom as well!

(Note: I later found out that Martha, the prayer leader, also had an abortion in her past, and was still struggling. She ended up going through a Surrendering the Secret healing retreat and becoming a co-facilitator!)

With my newfound freedom, I began to soar spiritually! I dove into the Word and sought Him with my whole heart. He ministered to me through His perfect love.

"And we, who with unveiled faces all reflect the Lord's glory, are being transformed into his likeness with ever-increasing glory, which comes from the Lord, who is the Spirit." II Corinthians 3:18

But, my courage to share my secret faded and I didn't tell

anyone else. Fear kept my mouth bound.

In February 2000, I missed my period. I couldn't believe it. A few months earlier, I was sure that God told me our family was complete, so I shifted my thinking in that direction, and focused on raising our four growing children.

So, needless to say, we were in shock…and denial. The enemy even whispered in my ear that maybe I would miscarry this baby. Entangled by that fear, we didn't tell anyone.

It wasn't until the end of the first trimester that we finally told our family and friends. Of course, they were happy for us, and the reality of having five kids, stretching our already thin budget, settled in. Joy, intermingled with the nagging fear that something may still happen to our baby, carried me through.

I read a book about supernatural childbirth, and desired to trust God for the promise of no labor pain during delivery. I studied the scriptures, spoke them out loud, and applied them to my life, believing that His Word is truth.

On September 30, my trust was put to the test as my labor began. I listened to worship music on my headphones, experiencing no pain, as I worshiped the Lord like I was the only one in the hospital room.

A few short hours later, with minimal pain during delivery, our precious Sarah Ann was born. I held our beautiful baby in my arms, my heart over-flowing with gratitude, the voices of doubt silenced. Not only had God kept his promise for a supernatural childbirth, but He extravagantly blessed us again with another child.

While we certainly did not deserve these gifts…having taken the life of our first child…in His abounding goodness and grace, He lavished His love upon us. Not because of who we are, but because of who He is.

Tim

During her supernatural labor and delivery, I was so proud of Debbie for standing so firmly on God's Word. The nurses and doctors were amazed as Debbie and I sat there praying and worshiping God.

The nurse and I watched the monitor spike to nine, ten, then off the paper as the contractions intensified, while Debbie continued to worship with a smile and no pain!

I believe God encouraged and built up the faith in everyone that was involved during Sarah's birth. Out of their mouths came words of complete amazement of never seeing anything like what they had just witnessed. Thank you, God for your grace and miracle working power!

December 25, 2000

Tim

That first Christmas as a family of seven, I must say I was feeling the pressure to provide a good Christmas for my family. I'm not going to lie. I was feeling like I was lacking in my duties as a provider, even though I was working full-time and doing everything I believed the Lord wanted me to do. I battled feelings of not being or doing good enough. I compared myself and my situation to others around me, listening to the negative voice of the evil one instead of believing what my Father God says about me.

I remember coming to the point of peace when I finally gave everything over to God, deciding to fully trust Him and not believe the lies.

This was our first Christmas celebrating at home by ourselves, and as a family of seven. Content and happy, it was a truly special time.

Our family Christmas tradition was to travel to Galesburg, where Debbie's sisters, their families and ours would gather in our childhood home with our parents, to celebrate Jesus' birth and enjoy family time together. Every year we would load up all the kids, suitcases and presents, and journey through the snow-covered roads, where we were met with hugs, kisses, and wonderful smells of baking cookies and banana bread.

Our oldest son, Christian, was 10, Kasey was 8, Kendall was 4, David was 22 months, and baby Sarah less than three months old. Debbie and I decided to stay home this Christmas. Breaking tradition was hard, especially for my people-pleasing wife, but it was the best decision for our family.

I remember stoking a fire in our wood-burning fireplace, as the seven of us gathered in our living room that Sunday night...Christmas Eve. We shared our gifts with each other and enjoyed quality time together.

The phone rang. I answered and a man's voice said, "Ho, Ho, Ho! Check your front porch."

We all looked at each other, mystified. I cautiously opened our front door, and there was a large, full, black garbage bag. I brought it inside and, to everyone's surprise, there were wrapped gifts, with each of our names on them! And not just one gift per person...two or three for each of us!

As we opened them, it was obvious that each gift was purchased specifically for each one of us: An Adidas wind-breaker suit for me (in my size), a gift certificate for an hour massage for Debbie, Razor scooter for Christian, fancy dress-up clothes for Kasey, cute clothes for Kendall, toddler musical instruments for David, a new outfit and baby items for Sarah!

Stunned, we thanked the Lord for blessing us in this special way.

Then the phone rang again. "Ho, Ho, Ho! Check your front porch again," said the same deep voice.

To everyone's delight, there on the porch was another large black bag full of gifts! How exciting it was for all of us to unwrap these gifts of love!

We sat there with our beautiful family, laughing and crying tears of joy!

As a father it was such a blessing to sit the kids down and explain to each of them that Jesus loved them. He loved us all so much that He gave us these gifts. To take the time to explain to them that as nice as these gifts were, and as much as we liked them, the birth of Jesus and His sacrifice was the greatest gift anyone could ever receive.

We still to this day do not know who our special Santa was that cold, winter night. But, we will always remember that Christmas miracle when God blessed us beyond our comprehension and will pass along this story to brag on God for generations to come.

Debbie

You may be wondering why stories like these are in a book about healing after abortion. We believe these are important to demonstrate how much God truly loves us, the depth of His love, and how He longs to lavish His love upon His children. Even though we don't deserve it. Even though we had sex before marriage and committed murder. Even though we lied to cover it up. Even though we believed Satan's lies more than God's truth. He still loves us the same.

There is nothing I can ever do to make God love me more or love me less. His perfect love is unfailing, unconditional, and extravagant! And, He is no respecter of persons, so these truths are the same for everyone.

8

Surrendering the Secret

February 2002

Debbie

As part of the leadership team at our church, Tim and I were asked to attend an Encounter weekend retreat, one weekend for the women and the next weekend for the men.

Three ladies trekked from Baton Rouge, Louisiana, to Carlinville, Illinois, to lead the women's retreat. I remember being totally transparent leading up to the weekend, and praying, *Lord, I give you permission to do whatever you want to do in me.*

When we arrived at the retreat center, we braced ourselves against the bitter cold wind, as we unloaded the cars and got settled in.

The leaders directed an extended time of worship and several teachings, before we all headed to bed.

In my dream that night, I was in the middle of a tug-of-war, not literally, but spiritually. It was good vs evil, tugging back and forth, fighting over me.

I woke up abrubtly with my stomach severely cramping.

Nausea and diarrhea forced me to camp out in the bathroom the majority of the night.

When morning finally came, I was too sick to get out of bed, and asked my roommate to let the leaders know I wouldn't be able to attend. Not long afterward, the ladies came to my room, prayed over me, and encouraged me to join them, if there was any way I could. I objected, not wanting to share my sick germs with everyone, and didn't feel like getting cleaned up. They insisted, assuring me they didn't care what I looked like and would have a puke bucket available if I needed it.

They understood the spiritual warfare at work, wreaking this havoc, and that if I took a step of faith to get there, God would meet me in a powerful way.

I weakly prayed for God to help me, dragged myself out of bed, and got dressed. I made it to the meeting room, a short distance away, and collapsed into a chair in the back of the room. Willing myself to stay awake and not to throw up, I struggled to concentrate on what was being taught.

I specifically remember one of the leaders talking about Jesus, in vivid detail, describing what he went through after he was betrayed in the Garden.

How he was beaten to the point of death, and scourged.

How the soldiers twisted together a crown of thorns and put it upon his head, and clothed him in a purple robe, mocking him over and over by saying, "Hail, King of the Jews!" while striking him in the face.

How the people rejected him and demanded that he be crucified.

How he, already so close to death, carried his own rough, heavy cross, to the place of the Skull.

How the soldiers hammered thick, long nails through

Jesus' wrists and feet, into the rugged wood of the cross, then lifted the cross, putting the post into the hole in the ground with a jolt.

How the religious leaders and soldiers sneered at him, spit on him, and turned their backs on him.

How Jesus spoke these words, "Father, forgive them, for they do not know what they are doing."

How Jesus breathed his last breath and died.

It was intense, as the somber reality of Jesus's suffering moved me deeply.

We were asked to step forward, one at a time. As I stood in front of the leader, she pressed a long, thick iron nail into my palm, and said, "It was your sin that put Jesus on the cross." That crushing truth hit me like a ton of bricks. Because of me, my sin, Jesus was tortured and crucified in such a brutal way. Because of my rebellion, and lies, and disobedience, and anger, and disrespect, and...murder...Jesus left heaven to come to this earth as a newborn baby, to die a criminal's death...to rescue me.

Through Jesus's death on the cross and miraculous resurrection three days later, the power of sin and death were conquered once and for all, creating a new covenant between God and man. The blood of Jesus was poured out for me, for the forgiveness of my sins. He did it all for me.

I was overcome with sorrow and cried out to God to forgive me for my sins. I withdrew to my chair, weeping at the realization of the depth of His love for me.

Next, we were taught about forgiveness, and the truths in God's word about holding grudges and unforgiveness in our hearts toward others, comparing it to drinking poison and expecting the other person to die. Unforgiveness destroys us from the inside out, and is a sin, as Jesus commands us to "forgive our trespasses, as we forgive those who trespass against us."

Having practiced this command throughout my life, I didn't have a long list of people to forgive. But, during those quiet moments of prayer and reflection, Holy Spirit revealed that I needed to forgive the person that suggested we get the abortion. I can honestly say I was not angry with this person, but it was important for me to speak those words of forgiveness, out loud, to release him in my spirit. In an act of obedience, I did.

Later that evening, there was a designated time to sit quietly before the Lord, to be still, and then approach the leaders when we were ready to be prayed for. By this time, I felt a little better, and just soaked in God's presence. I waited as each lady in our group walked forward to receive prayer. Then it was my turn.

As the leaders took turns praying out loud for me, I specifically remember them praying against the spirit of heaviness, the spirit of guilt and shame, commanding them to flee in the name of Jesus. No one in that room knew about the abortion, so these ladies knew nothing about me or my past. But God did. Holy Spirit pin-pointed exactly what needed to be prayed in order for these things to be broken off me.

This wasn't just a "Lord bless Debbie" prayer…it was warfare! They called upon the Lord with authority, to set me free from these spiritual bondages!

The power of God came upon me, and I began to weep. Hot tears poured out of me. The more they prayed, the harder I cried…and cried, and cried, and cried. It was if the toxic poison that had been locked up inside me for the past 15 years was finally being released and pouring out of me through my tears! I encountered the deepest cleansing of my life.

The weight of guilt and shame that ensnared me all those

years evaporated! I literally felt lighter!

I knew the chains had been broken off and I was free!!!

I am crying even now as I write this 17 years later as I remember, with gratitude, what God did in me that very moment...how powerfully His love broke the bonds of slavery, opened the prison doors, and walked me to freedom!!! Glory be to God, our Father!

Immediately, I felt compelled to share with the entire group about the abortion and the miracle that just occurred. The shackles of fear that kept me silent for one and a half decades were finally gone!

Not worrying about what the others would think of me, God gave me the boldness to break the silence, revealing my secret and breakthrough.

I'm sure the other attendees, most I had known for five years, were shocked to hear that I had an abortion, but they didn't show it. Instead, they embraced me with love and acceptance, further solidifying the work of Christ, dispelling the lies that others would reject me.

The leaders encouraged and challenged each of us to share our transformation testimonies as soon as possible, and as often as possible, citing Revelation 12:11,

"They overcame him by the blood of the Lamb and by the word of their testimony; they did not love their lives so much as to shrink from death."

Tim

While working full-time at IDOT, I completed online Bible classes, earned my pastoral certification, and served as part-time associate pastor at our church. Little did I know when Debbie left for that weekend retreat, that my wife would never be the same!

I remember their return that Sunday afternoon, where the men hosted a celebration service for the women who went on the retreat. As my wife climbed out of the church van, I could see a difference! She smiled like I had not seen in a long time. With her joy restored, happiness burst through her being.

We hugged and cried as she told me about the awesome miracle God had provided and that she no longer was in bondage and fear from the abortion. Wow…what an answer to prayer! I knew this was God!

Now remember, I served as one of the associate pastors…I had leadership responsibilities, and everyone knew Pastor Tim. So, I wasn't sure how everyone would react to this news…this intimate detail about our lives.

But, let me tell you, I could not have been any happier for my wife…she was set free and so was I!

Out of love for Debbie, I had kept our secret, not ever wanting to cause her more pain. But now, all bets were off! No more holding back. No more fear of people. Just a deep and pressing desire to say, "Yes" to God no matter what He wanted us to do.

The next weekend our pastor allowed Debbie to stand in front of the entire church on Sunday morning to share our testimony, how God transformed her at the retreat, removing all her guilt and shame.

I remember thinking as she walked up to the front to share, *This is real. I'm one of the pastors of these people and everyone is about to know something so intimate about us.* But, I did not care.

As I sat and watched as she unveiled the details, I remember crying and being overwhelmed with thankfulness to the Lord that He made us whole again.

She glowed as the Holy Spirit engulfed her and spoke

through her with sweet words. Words of encouragement for others to accept the gift of forgiveness and healing from our Heavenly Father for whatever it was in their lives the devil was using to keep them separated from God.

With great power, she testified of God's goodness, letting everyone know He is no respecter of persons. What He had done for us, He would do for them.

As she stood there in humility, the Lord revealed that my wife was unrobing the shame.

Never again would she wear that cloak or be burdened by that sin.

Words cannot express my thanks to God for extending such a sweet gift...my wife made whole again!

Our pastor then gave an altar call for anyone who had something in their past that was holding them back or keeping them from drawing closer to God, inviting them to come forward. Let me tell you, the altars were full! Men and women alike came forward, not all looking for healing from a past abortion, but seeking God's forgiveness for their secret sins, that only God knew about. We prayed with every person and God performed miracles that day.

I for one have never been the same.

Debbie

After service, women and men approached me, amazed at what God had done. With a seemingly heavy heart, one gentleman said, "It must feel incredible to have that weight lifted off of you." I soon realized that I was not alone in carrying the weight of guilt and shame. It affects everyone, regardless of the sin committed. The enemy uses it as a weapon against us, holding us hostage from the love and forgiveness of God.

Now that we surrendered our secret, it was important for me and Tim to tell our families. We knew God was asking us to share our story openly, and we would not have the freedom to do that if we kept this from our families. Knowing that the service was recorded and would later be televised, we were concerned about our family finding out before we got a chance to tell them in person.

We started with our children, who ranged in age from 11 years to 18 months old, by sharing age-appropriate details, focusing on God's forgiveness and healing. Our children loved us unconditionally.

Our parents and siblings were next. That was the hardest part for me…telling my Mom and Dad. I did not want to hurt them, or any of our family members, but couldn't keep this in the dark any longer. We trusted Holy Spirit to minister to their hearts.

I remember sitting around our dining room table at our home, with my Mom and Dad and two sisters, during their next visit to Springfield. Overcoming intense fear, God's grace abounded as Tim and I honestly divulged details about the pregnancy, abortion and the healing miracle I received.

My dad cried. As a man of few words, who didn't cry often, I asked him why he was crying. Between sobs he lamented, "I'm sorry you had to go through all of that on your own. That you felt like you couldn't come to us." I suddenly realized he wasn't crying because he was mad or disappointed in me, as I expected. He was crying because he was sad that he wasn't there for me during such a difficult time. That he didn't get the chance to protect his daughter. That we felt too scared to tell them for 15 years. Wow. What a beautiful expression of my father's unconditional love and forgiveness.

Gripped with sadness, my mom cried too. She later wrote,

"We were shocked, in disbelief and sad, with many tears being shed. Even though we were hurting, we could see they were hurting, and we loved and supported them. I felt I hadn't done a good job as a Mom and I questioned God if it was partly my fault. He assured me that, no, it was not my fault." They both dealt with it by not talking about it and not telling anyone.

Several years later, Mom shared how she had to work through sadness with the Lord. Sadness that I struggled through the ectopic scare all alone. And deep sorrow for the loss of her grandchild.

She wrestled to forgive us. And struggled to tell her friends, as most of them were from the same church I grew up in. She recently wrote, "I really didn't know what their reaction would be but was blessed and surprised by their positive and supportive attitude. Not one person had a condemning word. I was very much relieved and felt a weight lifted off which freed me to not feel shame."

God faithfully carried her through those rough times, comforting her through the sadness, empowering her to extend forgiveness, and expose the secret. "We are thankful to know that Jesus has their little one in His arms."

Isn't it such an evil ploy how the enemy even lied to my mom, attacking her security as a mother, weighing her down with shame, and telling her that this was somehow her fault? This is one testament of how abortion impacts more than just the mother, father and baby. The negative ripple effect on others is far-reaching.

Thankfully, my sisters also wrapped their arms around us, in love and forgiveness. Relieved, Tim and I thanked God for giving us the courage to take these first steps of obedience.

Tim

Revealing our secret to Debbie's family was one of the hardest things I have ever had to do. Her parents entrusted their daughter to me and I let them down. For that, I was heartbroken. We all cried together, embracing the truth that they were grandparents and aunts to our child in heaven. Because of God's favor and mercy, forgiveness was extended as the result of our obedience.

To expose to my parents and family that I had committed this sin of abortion was not easy. You see, currently there are over 120 people in my father's bloodline. So, having a family is a big deal and part of a deep and lasting heritage I do not take lightly.

My parents received the news with a heavy heart, along with my brothers and sisters, but each one offered love, support and forgiveness. For that I will forever be grateful.

Several of them tell our story to encourage people to find healing from whatever it is that keeps them shackled to their past. That is a miracle in itself! God transforms what was meant for our harm and turns it into a blessing. Thank you, Jesus!

9

On the Move

8 months later - October 2002

Debbie

Living in a 1200 square foot home, with three bedrooms and one bathroom (emphasis on one), was no longer working for our growing family. Not only did we have 5 children, but they were growing, causing our home to bust at the seams! Tim and I prayed for nearly three years asking God to provide the right home, in the right location, at the right time. We wrote our list of things we were believing for in our new home: plenty of land and space for the kids to safely play outside (not on a busy road), five bedrooms, three bathrooms, central air, large kitchen with a window above the sink, and located to the east/northeast of Springfield.

Tim

I came across a newspaper ad for a big house in the country. It sounded great, until I noticed the address. I was disappointed knowing it was completely the opposite direction to where we believed God was going to put us. I mean, my work and our church were located on the far side of town from this house. I remember hearing the Lord speak into my heart to drive out by the house, so I did.

As I pulled up and slowly drove by, I noticed it was an old school house with a big yard and lots of room for the kids. In my spirit I believed this was going to be our new home. All I had to do now was tell Debbie.

After a little persuasion from me, but mostly from the Holy Spirit, Debbie agreed, and we set an appointment to walk through the house.

This house was amazing! With over 4000 square feet, everything on our list (and more) was in this house, including the central air system, which was installed merely weeks before our showing! And the owners were so warm and friendly. They later told us they were praying for a large, Christian family to purchase their beloved home. We left believing this house was for us, for the next season of our lives.

I was spending time in prayer that next week and the Lord told me to write the owner of the house a letter to share the things the Lord would reveal to me.

Needless to say, I was a little fearful and taken back, but I wanted to trust Him. I believed in Him more than the fear, so I started to write. God gave me a word of knowledge for this man and his family; things that only he and the Lord knew about. I wrote down everything I believed God wanted to say to them through me. At the end, I wrote, "I know this letter may seem strange to you, but I had to be obedient to the Lord. And I figured you would either think I'm totally crazy or I believed what I was saying." I also wrote the amount the Lord gave me to offer for the house; $14,000 less than the asking price.

Impressed to hand-deliver the letter, the following Sunday

afternoon I drove out to drop it off. No one was home so I left it in the door and believed for the best. Later that night I received a call from the home owner. I said, "Hello," but it was quiet on the other end. So, I repeated my greeting. With a broken voice, he said, "Hello, Tim."

He thanked me for the letter and confirmed that the things written were spot on. This confirmation not only built his faith, but mine as well. God cared enough about this man's broken heart that He used me, a perfect stranger, to reveal these things to him. I was blown away.

At the end of our conversation, he agreed to our offer with no counter offer!

A month later at the closing, Debbie and I found a seat at the long conference room table, across from the banker. Moments later, as the owners of the house entered, we jumped to our feet to offer warm hugs and greetings. As we signed the stack of paperwork, we joked and teased each other, our laughter and excitement filling the room. With a chuckle, the banker commented that this kind of transaction was not normal! Most people don't have this kind of relationship when buying and selling a house.

Our hearts are full of thankfulness as we remember these demonstrations of God's extravagant love and generosity toward our family.

10

My Life Calling

Debbie

Not long after my transformative encounter with the Lord, God showed me a vision. I wasn't sleeping so it wasn't a dream. I was meditating on God's Word and praying when this picture appeared in my mind.

There before me appeared a sea of women, as far as I could see, and Holy Spirit spoke gently to me, *All these women are hurting from the pain of abortion and I want to use you to help them find healing.*

Woah. What a humbling moment.

Awe set in as I grasped how clearly Holy Spirit spoke to me, and the gravity of this mission, this calling. This image is forever etched on my heart and mind.

I can hear those words just as clearly today as I did that memorable day in 2002.

Armed with this new sense of purpose and excited to get started, questions - actually prayers - quickly arose. *How do you want me to accomplish this, Lord? What's my first step?*

After months of prayer…no clear answer. But, I did feel a nudge to contact the local pregnancy center to see if I could volunteer in some way.

During my interview, the Director asked me to elaborate about my abortion experience and healing. Sharing with confidence and boldness, I revealed in detail how God healed my broken heart and set me free. Moved by my story, she believed the best role for me to serve in would be a peer counselor, to minister directly to the clients who walked in our doors looking for help.

I enjoyed serving in that capacity for two and a half years, sharing options information, pregnancy and parenting education, and the good news of Jesus with each vulnerable mother.

I planned to continue volunteering there, until God impressed upon me to step down. I was confused. *But, isn't this what you have called me to do?* He made it very clear that my time there was complete.

In August 2006, our youngest daughter, Sarah, was getting ready to start Kindergarten. Having been a stay-at-home Mom for 14 years, I had dreams of relaxing and soaking in some "Me" time when all our kids were finally in school. Shopping, laying in the sun, exercising consistently, taking long walks, enjoying long uninterrupted naps (oh yeah!), and curling up on the couch with a good book…all by myself.

Well, God had other plans! After I resigned (an act of obedience), He instructed me to spend quality and quantity time alone with Him every morning.

So, after bag lunches were made, homework tucked into book bags, and kisses to the youngest ones boarding the bus, my mission was to have Time Alone With God. TAWG. Yep, God took me back to the basics, just as He did during those quiet moments under the tree at youth camp.

He extended freedom for me to choose how to share this

time with Him, anything from reading my Bible or other Christian books, journaling, dancing around my living room to my favorite worship music, laying on the floor soaking in the stillness of His presence, basking in the warm sunshine as I walked along our country roads, or simply talking and listening to Jesus.

So, every morning, I had a date. And every morning, God was faithful to meet me there. Rarely did I miss our date.

This time wasn't always pleasant, though. It was what I call a spiritual boot camp. This was dig deep time.

As I dedicated this intentional "no agenda" time, weeks turned into months, and as a result, my spiritual roots deepened...roots of faith and trust in God.

I learned to study His Word in depth, digging for hidden treasures I didn't know were there, not just reading a verse here or there. He stretched me beyond my comfort zone, challenging me to be still (and that's not easy for a Mom of five active kids) and to discern His voice more clearly. I gained understanding about my identity in Christ and the authority He has given me. My faith grew. My confidence soared. The old mindsets and traditions of men were being stripped away and torn down and being re-built on the strong foundation of God's Word.

May 2007

Debbie

After 9 months of boot camp, I was helping lead an Encounter retreat, when one of my co-leaders whispered during prayer time, "God wants to tell you something." As I quietly laid on the floor in His peaceful presence, Holy Spirit spoke gently into my spirit, *It's time. I have chosen you. You can say no and I will find someone else, but I have chosen you.*

Woah! Another defining moment in my life!

While God didn't reveal what it was time for, I knew what He meant. The past few months, I had been sensing a leading to open a pregnancy center in Springfield. A pregnancy center reaches out to women and men making difficult pregnancy decisions (like me and Tim), transforming their fears into confidence, and empowering them to make healthy, life-affirming decisions. And now, that calling was confirmed! Ignorant about how to start a pregnancy center and with $0 to fund it, Tim and I said, "Yes!" trusting in God's provision.

One reason I needed this confirmation was because there was already a pregnancy center in Springfield (the one I volunteered at), so I didn't want to step on anyone's toes (people-pleasing spirit still rearing its ugly head). But, once I had that word from the Lord, it was full steam ahead (God-pleaser!).

Another confirmation I realized later, was the timing. Did you catch that a few paragraphs ago? It had been 9 months of spiritual boot camp when the calling was spoken...*9 months.* The length of a pregnancy! And now God chose us to help women making difficult pregnancy decisions!

It was as if the calling was conceived in me last August when boot camp started, with the vision growing steadily in my spirit throughout that time, then was birthed at that May encounter! I don't believe in coincidences...only God-incidences! Only He can put the intricate puzzle pieces together so perfectly.

Tim and I prayed about what to name this new ministry, and landed on Lifetime Pregnancy Help Center, based on Psalm 30:5,

"For his anger lasts only a moment, but his favor lasts a *lifetime*; weeping may remain for a night, but rejoicing comes in the morning." (Emphasis mine)

That's the promise for every believer…a lifetime of God's favor! And that was our vision and desire for our clients.

Armed with only a name and a sure calling, Tim and I shared our vision with our church body. The love and support showered upon us fueled our passion! Our friends and people we didn't even know caught the vision and rallied around us with enthusiastic support.

Tim

When Debbie relayed the powerful word God spoke to her, I believe the Lord revealed that my job was to do whatever I could to make sure she was out front telling our story and helping others find freedom and healing.

I prayed, *Lord, what does that look like?*

God said, *For starters, trust Me fully and resign from your associate pastor post.*

It was very hard to walk into our pastor's office and resign, and humbling, but I knew God had something more for us and wanted to use us in a new and exciting way, so I said, "Yes."

This new season as a family began with $0 to invest into the ministry and just $400 a month of stable family income! Let me tell you, with five growing kids and a wife, $400 does not stretch very far!

It wasn't long before God's provision started to manifest in different ways, showering us with His goodness for both our family and the ministry. I'm so thankful Debbie and I were unified and believed together as we took a huge risk, stepping out of the boat by faith.

It is awesome to wake up every day and know what my calling is; to know what God wants me to do. Saving the lives of babies, women and men is what God requires of us and we are humbled to accept the call.

July 2, 2007

Debbie

Our first day as a ministry, I sat in Tim's former office and prayed for wisdom and direction regarding what steps to take to see this vision become a reality. Tim nor I had ever done anything like this before…no prior experience or training…simply a word from the Lord and passion to fulfill our destiny and see His Kingdom advanced. So, I needed guidance.

One of the first things I did was to call other similar non-profit organizations in Springfield, as well as other pregnancy centers throughout Illinois. While most people greeted me warmly and listened respectfully as I shared the vision, one woman was definitely not happy about this news.

I distinctly remember her saying, "There is no money here. We have to fundraise in Chicago for our support. And abortion is not an issue in Springfield. I can count on two hands how many women we have seen in the past 25+ years that wanted an abortion."

Stunned, I politely thanked her for her time and ended the call. I paused and prayed at that very moment against the lies of the enemy and this spiritual attack on our calling. Satan used this woman to try to create fear and doubt regarding God's word and promises, and I wasn't going to let him! I did not allow those darts to penetrate my heart or spirit and trusted the armor I was wearing to protect me. Peace quickly came.

Just a few hours later, a woman from our church called about a friend's daughter who was pregnant and was considering abortion. Wow…Talk about a quick answer to prayer! Not that I was happy that this young girl was pregnant or considering abortion, but thankful to God for confirming the vision yet again, that abortion is a serious threat in our city, further sealing the calling in my spirit.

Concerned about this young mom and her dire situation, I called the friend to offer encouragement, referrals and prayer regarding her daughter.

Our very first day of ministry, and God distinctly solidified our purpose.

One month later

Debbie

Back to those stellar church friends and family: Tim and I decided to host a Walk fundraiser to generate revenue to propel the ministry forward. On August 4, nearly 100 men, women and children rallied together at Lincoln Park in Springfield to walk one mile with us. Fifty-six fundraisers turned in their pledge forms, along with cash and checks they collected. To our amazement, those 56 people raised over $15,000!!! Holy cow! We were overwhelmed and humbled by God's incredible out-pouring of funds AND friends for the ministry. People who believed in the vision and partnered with us to see it come alive! And, yet another confirmation of His promise to provide financially.

As a result, our newly formed Board of Directors agreed to begin paying me a modest salary for my role as Director, a huge blessing for our family!

We held a second fundraiser in the Spring of 2008, a

banquet, to further establish our finances and secure much-needed monthly support. Again, God blew us away by pouring out His provision of over $46,000 through 155 generous people who captured and embraced the vision that night!

This foundational support funded our lease (and later purchase) of a building, actually a homey house that was already zoned for medical purposes.

We officially opened our doors October 20, 2008, offering self-administered pregnancy tests, options information, on-going pregnancy and parenting support, community referrals and abortion recovery support groups (more about those in Chapter 13).

There are literally dozens of stories I could highlight, demonstrating God's incredible favor, provision, and power in transforming lives through this ministry.

Since those humble beginnings, the ministry has grown exponentially. Here are just a few examples: a name change to First Step Women's Center; expanded services to a medical facility to include pregnancy testing, ultrasound, Sexually Transmitted Disease testing and treatment, options consultations; a new state-of-the-art Mobile Medical Unit to take our life-saving services to vulnerable women throughout our community; and most recently, the purchase of and move to a 8,500 square foot building, enabling us to serve three times the number of patients.

God has been so faithful every step of the way.... not because of who we are, but because of who He is!

11

Like an Onion

Debbie

While my freedom may seem like it happened all at once, it was actually a series of encounters that I experienced before and after that weekend retreat. Many times, our healing comes in layers, like an onion. As we surrender new territory to Him, He meets us right there, at that point of surrender. When we've conquered that territory through Christ, He leads us to the next point of surrender. It's a journey. And the good news is that He is with us every step of the way.

On my journey, I believe my first point of surrender was asking God to forgive me for having sex outside of His perfect will, and for taking the life of our child. True to His Word, He forgave me.

He then began building a new foundation of trust: trust in Him and trust in Tim. He tore out the old "stuff" and, brick by brick, He taught me through His Word and everyday life experiences how to trust Him. He demonstrated His faithfulness to me over and over, proving His true character.

As this foundation was strengthened, He revealed that I needed to forgive myself for the abortion, to fully embrace what Jesus did through His death and resurrection. As I humbly prayed that simple prayer, He again was right there, leading me through the rubble of the collapsed wall, into the next leg of the journey.

Then came the encounter weekend, when the shackles fell off, the prison doors flung open, and He walked me out of the captivity of guilt and shame for good! But, that wasn't the end of the journey!

About five years after the retreat, our pastor invited people to worship and pray every evening leading up to Easter together at the church. There was no structured service. Just quiet worship music playing as people prayed. My husband's beautiful voice broke the silence as he sang, "As far as the east is from the west," a popular song by Chris Tomlin, based on Psalm 103:11-12,

> "For as high as the heavens are above the earth, so great is his love for those who fear him; as far as the east is from the west, so far has he removed our transgressions from us."

I remember standing near the altar, soaking in God's sweet presence, my heart so full of gratitude for the transformation in my life.

I opened my eyes for just a moment, and on the large video screen above the stage, a picture of a baby's hand resting in the palm of a father's hand moved me deeply. I closed my eyes, and thanked God for that visual reminder that my aborted baby was safe with Him.

Suddenly, a picture appeared in my mind, one could say it was a vision, of Jesus sitting, holding two babies on His lap. He spoke lovingly, *This is Thomas and Abigail. They are here with me and are safe and loved. They love you and are not mad at you.*

Wow!!! Talk about water works! Not only did God brand another incredible visual on my spirit, but Jesus named my children for me! Thomas…the baby we aborted, and Abigail…the baby we miscarried.

I didn't even know I should name them. And these are not names I would have chosen. I inscribed other potential baby names in the back of my Bible over the years, but these two were the names Jesus chose for them! He not only revealed their names, but their gender.

Overwhelmed by the immense value God placed on my children, and by the depth of His love for me, I fell to my knees and wept. He loves me so unconditionally that He would give me such a precious gift! With unworthiness gone, I embraced this gift and His extravagant love!

We no longer refer to our babies as the one we aborted and the one we miscarried. Rather, they are Thomas and Abigail, members of our family, who we long to see and hold when we enter those pearly gates in heaven.

III.

There Is Hope

12

Extravagant Love

Debbie

While the specific details may be different, our story is not unique. With over 62 million abortions performed in the U.S. since abortion was legalized in 1973, there are millions of hurting women and men, many suffering in silent pain, like we were.

Women and men who are struggling to carry the same heavy baggage I was carrying...

...believing the same condemning lies
...buried in heaps of shame, guilt, unworthiness
...shackled to the prison of their past
...isolated in their suffering.

A profound number of women have experienced other difficulties that I did not personally deal with, as a result of abortion trauma, such as:

+ serious physical complications
+ infertility
+ drug and/or alcohol addictions
+ Post-Traumatic Stress Disorder (PTSD)
+ depression

+ anxiety
+ mental health issues
+ suicidal thoughts and behaviors
+ inability to bond with later children
+ being an extremely over-protective parent
+ self-hatred
+ sexual dysfunction
+ flashbacks
+ chronic crying
+ sleep disorders
…to name a few.

Still others have had multiple abortions, which adds more layers of repercussions. (For more information about the effects of abortion, visit The Elliot Institute at www.afterabortion.org)

If you've had an abortion or abortions, and you recognize even one of these symptoms in your life, there is hope. God desires to meet you right where you are and walk with you through your healing journey to set you free!

Contrary to the lie Satan tries to engrave on our minds, abortion is not the unforgivable sin. It is the shedding of innocent blood, and God hates that sin, according to Proverbs 6:17. But He loves us as His creation and sent His Son, Jesus, to be the sacrificial lamb to cover our sin. Big difference. God hates our sin, but He loves us. Let that sink in.

When steeped in the deception of the enemy, it's easy to hear those words, but hard to embrace them. We may even share about God's love with someone who's hurting, but our insecurity and unworthiness causes us to reject that for ourselves. We sometimes believe the fullness of God's love and blessings is for others, but not for us.

This is a ploy of Satan to keep us trapped, imprisoned if

you will, to our past, keeping us from receiving the extravagant love and blessings of our Father.

God cares about every detail in your life. Because of His unfailing love, He sent his Son, Jesus, to this earth, to suffer and die, taking my sin and your sin to the grave, so that we can be resurrected, just as He was!

These words were prophesied about Jesus in Isaiah 61 many years before his birth,

"The Spirit of the Sovereign Lord is on me, because the Lord has anointed me to proclaim good news to the poor. He has sent me to **bind up the brokenhearted,** to **proclaim freedom for the captives and release from darkness for the prisoners**, to proclaim the year of the Lord's favor and the day of vengeance of our God, **to comfort all who mourn,** and **provide for those who grieve** in Zion— **to bestow on them a crown of beauty instead of ashes, the oil of joy instead of mourning, and a garment of praise instead of a spirit of despair.** They will be called oaks of righteousness, a planting of the Lord for the display of his splendor. They will rebuild the ancient ruins and restore the places long devastated; they will renew the ruined cities that have been devastated for generations. Strangers will shepherd your flocks; foreigners will work your fields and vineyards. And you will be called priests of the Lord, you will be named ministers of our God. You will feed on the wealth of nations, and in their riches you will boast. **Instead of your shame you will receive a double portion, and instead of disgrace you will rejoice in your inheritance. And so you**

will inherit a double portion in your land, and everlasting joy will be yours." (Emphasis mine)

Wow! What powerful words written for you and for me!

God desires to heal your broken heart and shower you with His love. He gives you permission to grieve the loss of your child(ren) and promises to comfort you while you grieve. He wants to "bestow on (you) a crown of beauty instead of ashes, the oil of gladness instead of mourning, and a garment of praise instead of a spirit of despair." Jesus has come "…to proclaim freedom for the captives and release from darkness for the prisoners…"

The Bible tells us about a man named Daniel, who was thrown into a den of lions as punishment, and how no man could save him, not even the King. Daniel trusted God to protect him, and the mouths of the lions were miraculously closed! Here's what the King said about God after Daniel was pulled safely from the den,

> "For he is the living God and he endures forever; his kingdom will not be destroyed, his dominion will never end. **He rescues and he saves;** he performs signs and wonders in the heavens and on the earth. He has rescued Daniel from the power of the lions." Daniel 6:26-27 (Emphasis mine)

Figuratively, are you in a lion's den right now? A deep pit of despair, fear, shame, self-destruction, broken relationships, emptiness, loneliness, guilt, unworthiness, self-loathing, anger or hopelessness, with the enemy prowling around, threatening your life?

God will meet you right where you are…in that pit. No

need to try to scratch and claw your way out only to fall to the pit floor. Or clean up first. Or try to get a handle on things yourself or be embarrassed by the mess you've made. He wants to reach down into that pit and rescue you! To pull you out of the darkness into His wonderful light. Why? Because He loves you!

God loves you because He created you. The psalmist declares in Psalm 139,

"For you created my inmost being; you knit me together in my mother's womb. I praise you because I am fearfully and wonderfully made;…"

"My frame was not hidden from you when I was made in the secret place. When I was woven together in the depths of the earth, your eyes saw my unformed body. All the days ordained for me were written in your book before one of them came to be."

Because of His unconditional love for you, God sent His only Son, Jesus, to die on the cross to pay for your sin.

"For God so loved the world that he gave his one and only Son, that whoever believes in him shall not perish but have eternal life. For God did not send his Son into the world to condemn the world, but to save the world through him." John 3:16-17

If you have never surrendered your life to God, or maybe you have walked away from Him, this may be your time. You have done all you can do to fix yourself and may be exhausted from trying.

Simply lift your arms in the air as a symbolic act of surrender to God, (like the universal sign for "I give up" or like a child, "Pick me up") and pray a sincere prayer from your heart. Acknowledge that you have sinned against Him and ask Him to forgive you. Surrender your life to Him, inviting Him to take control, to lift you out of the pit. Then receive His love and forgiveness, because what He did on the cross was enough.

Here are some verses to guide your prayer:

"...for all have sinned and fall short of the glory of God..." Romans 3:23

"For the wages of sin is death, but the gift of God is eternal life in Christ Jesus our Lord." Romans 6:23

"But God demonstrates his own love for us in this: While we were still sinners, Christ died for us." Romans 5:8

"Jesus answered, 'I am the way and the truth and the life. No one comes to the Father except through me.'" John 14:6

"That if you confess with your mouth, 'Jesus is Lord,' and believe in your heart that God raised him from the dead, you will be saved. For it is with your heart that you believe and are justified, and it is with your mouth that you confess and are saved. As the Scripture says, 'Anyone who trusts in him will never be put to shame.' For there is no difference between Jew and Gentile — the same Lord is Lord of all and richly blesses all who call on him, for, 'Everyone who calls on the name of the Lord will be saved.'" Romans 10:9-13

"If we confess our sins, he is faithful and just and will forgive us our sins and purify us from all unrighteousness." I John 1:9

"And he died for all, that those who live should no longer live for themselves but for him who died for them and was raised again." II Corinthians 5:15

If you prayed a prayer of surrender for the first time or as a re-dedication of your life to Christ, we rejoice with you! You have received the free gift of eternal life with our Savior! Hallelujah!

His promises and blessings as detailed in His Word are for you!

"So if the Son sets you free, you will be free indeed." John 8:36

"Therefore, if anyone is in Christ, he is a new creation; the old has gone, the new has come!" II Corinthians 5:17

"Here I am! I stand at the door and knock. If anyone hears my voice and opens the door, I will come in and eat with him, and he with me." Revelation 3:20

"...I will never leave you nor forsake you." Joshua 1:5

"Be strong and courageous, because you will lead these

people to inherit the land I swore to their ancestors to give them. Be strong and very courageous. Be careful to obey all the law my servant Moses gave you; do not turn from it to the right or to the left, that you may be successful wherever you go. Do not let this Book of the Law depart from your mouth; meditate on it day and night, so that you may be careful to do everything written in it. Then you will be prosperous and successful. Have I not commanded you? Be strong and courageous. Do not be terrified; do not be discouraged, for the LORD your God will be with you wherever you go." Joshua 1:6-9

"Trust in the LORD with all your heart and lean not on your own understanding; in all your ways acknowledge him, and he will make your paths straight." Proverbs 3:5-6

These are just a few of God's promises we can trust and stand upon! I encourage you to read the book of John in the Bible to learn as much about Jesus as you can. Ask God to open your eyes and heart to His truths, then let His Word wash over you.

I encourage you to tell one person you trust about your decision to accept Christ's love and forgiveness. And to find a group of people, maybe a church or small group, who are wholeheartedly walking with God to link arms with you along this new journey.

Also, will you please take a few minutes to contact us to let us know a little about your story and of your decision to follow Christ? We would be thrilled to hear from you! (See back cover for contact info)

Tim

Yes, men…healing is for us as well. God desires for us all to be whole and feel His overwhelming love for us. Surrendering our pain and disappointment and allowing God to make us new transforms our outlook on everything.

We must stop believing the lies of the enemy that we are ok. To just keep our mouth shut, all the while holding onto our pain. To just keep moving on, never allowing anyone…much less God…help us.

The greatest decision I ever made was surrendering to Jesus and daily building a real and lasting relationship with Him. Embracing the understanding that He is for me and not against me brought such freedom.

The truth is that real men love Jesus and pursue His teachings. Even when we stumble and fail Him, breaking His heart with our sinful acts, He still wants the best for us. He still wants us to ask Him for help and forgiveness. When we as men start pursuing this kind of relationship with God, nothing is impossible. The Word of God is very clear in Proverbs 18:21, *"The tongue has the power of life and death…"*

Men, it is time to start speaking life into our relationships, into our workplaces, into our communities of influence. It's ok to let others see you fail, but it is most important to let others see how you respond to those failures. Let them see you ask someone you have wronged for forgiveness. Let others see you praying for your family and teaching them the truths of Jesus and His way.

Until we decide to put Jesus first, we will always be lacking in the things that truly matter. I encourage you to read the Scriptures above and speak them over yourself and your family and friends. It's time for men to rise up and speak life, and let God restore us to newness in Him.

Please join me in seeking after Jesus and doing whatever He requires of us. I truly believe we will see great and mighty things as renewal sweeps the land. As God the Father is restored back to His rightful place as King of Kings!

Poem by Tim Shultz

Listen, can you hear?
Look, can you see?
He is all around,
Yet lives inside of me.

Where can I go
That He's not already been?
My source and my shield,
Until the very end!

He is all I need,
No matter where I am;
When the storms of life rage on,
He whispers peace to me within.

There's no one like Him,
He bears my heavy load,
So I give it all to Him,
Because He loves me as His own.

Jesus paid it all,
So all to Him I give;
This life is not my own,
I lay it down for Him.

13

Breaking the Chains

Debbie

No matter where you are on your healing journey after abortion, if you are ready to trust God and take the next step, we would love to guide you. Please contact us. We truly want to help.

One of the ways we reach out to hurting women is to offer caring support through small groups...safe places free of judgment or condemnation. During these groups, we link arms and walk through the steps to healing...together. We study God's Word, finding truth to replace the lies.

Women around the world are being set free from their shameful past. Women held captive for several decades but were ready to let God minister to the deepest wounds of their broken hearts. The power of God moves mountains of deceit, unbelief, insecurity, and fear, and does exactly what He said in Isaiah 61...He sets the captives free!

I have been extremely blessed to facilitate a small group retreat including two to four courageous women several times each year and am continually amazed at the depth of God's grace and love He showers upon each one. How He meets us right where we are, in our brokenness, our pain, our entanglements, our neediness. How His Word comes to life as His truth washes our minds and spirits, bringing light into some very dark areas of our belief systems. It tears down strongholds and builds new foundations based on His truth.

Here's what several of these ladies shared after attending a group:

"God was right there with me revealing His love for me, His forgiveness, and His never-ending mercy. He truly transformed my heart of stone toward my abortion to a heart set free to acknowledge and remember my child without guilt, shame, and fear. God does perform miracles! Glory be to God!" Julie

"Several weeks before I attended the Forgiven and Set Free weekend, I talked about the abortion that I had over 25 years earlier for only the second time. I knew I was forgiven, and I thought I had dealt with the many issues related to the abortion. As we worked through the Bible study that weekend, I found even more forgiveness for myself and others that were involved. I also found healing from the wounds of abortion that I didn't even know I had. Now I know that I am truly forgiven and set free from the bondage of the memory of abortion." Sue

"The pain of abortion is compounded because it's the secret sin, the one you can't talk about, even to your friends. It's that very secret that keeps millions of women like me, and possibly you, suffering in silence. I had an abortion when I was 20 years old. For years, I didn't understand that I had buried the grief and the pain. Yes, you might say I had caused my own grief, but as I looked at the story of Jesus and the Woman at the Well (John 4:1-29), I could take comfort in the fact that although He knew her sin, he offered her restoration, and a drink of living water.

Surrendering the Secret was part of the plan that God used to help in the healing process. What began as an 8-week class, turned into a journey of healing and the beginning of lasting friendships. The class facilitators provided the perfect atmosphere of truth balanced with unconditional love.

I believe God has a mighty work for each of his children to accomplish. We are not disqualified by our sin. We are perhaps humbled by it and repentant for it, and yes, we may continue to reap some consequences of the events we started when we chose abortion, but we as mothers, feel the loss most keenly. We are, however, not as those who have no hope. We'll see our children in heaven.

Take heart. Our sins are forgiven. What Jesus did on the cross is big enough for this sin too. It's not too big to be covered in the blood. He died for you and me, that nothing would ever separate us from the love of the Father." Robin

One of our participants, Katie, wrote a moving poem after her retreat to express her healing journey and gratitude:

"Thunder crashes and lightening streaks across the sky.
Wind whips salty sea water up into a wall that seems impenetrable.
A boat drifts through the dark, open ocean with no hope of rescue.

Then, in the distance there is light.
Reaching, waiting, bright.
A light that restores hope to the boat and draws it near.
A light that loves and casts out fear.

What matters not is where the boat was going.
What matters not is where the boat has been.
What matters not is what the boat was doing.
What matters now is that the boat drifts in.

The vessel approaches, weary, worn, and battered.
Scared from the journey and afraid its sails are tattered.
Worried that the hull is broken beyond repair,
And ready to give up, its heart is drained of care.

But the light that comes from the cliffs above falls like a warm embrace.
Love, support, and comfort fill every empty space.
Repairs are made and holes are sealed.
The boat has scars, but it is healed.

A new course has been set and a new guide leads the way.
Faith, hope, and love are fueling this new day.
With the sun on the horizon, and a gentle breeze,
The wonderfully and beautifully made boat sails the open seas.

Thank you for being a lighthouse and allowing God's light to shine
from within, bright and reaching out over the open sea."

Amen and amen! God's unconditional love is for Julie, for Sue, for Robin, for Katie, for me and for you!

I hope these testimonies encourage you to take the next step of faith and give you peace to know that God will meet you as you step toward Him.

There are many excellent resources available to help you take the next step. I recommend several on the last pages of this book.

Tim

Abortion recovery ministry is not only necessary for women. It is also needed for men. Since men are always part of the events that lead to pregnancy, and many times are the ones who put pressure on women (directly or indirectly) to have the abortion, healing is needed.

I also understand that some men had no say at all in the abortion decision the women they were involved with made. I'm sure that pain is unbearable and extremely hard to carry and come to terms with.

I firmly believe that when men rise up and start to accept our role in the abortion and seek to receive healing, we will see a resurgence in the leadership that this country truly needs today.

I believe a great army of men and women who will find forgiveness and healing will rise up and take back what the devil has stolen. Take back broken and severed relationships. Take back places of honor and leadership that is lacking in many communities today.

I believe restoring the father is the first step in restoring the family, and from that we will see a great revival of restoration in our towns and cities in every community around this great country.

Maybe you are one of the wounded men searching for something. I believe God and His unfailing love is that something you are looking for.

"But seek first his kingdom and his righteousness, and all these things will be given to you as well." Matthew 6:33

14

Our Mission:

To help women and men embrace grace, heal, and
find freedom after abortion.

Debbie

In early 2019, God snapped another piece of our life puzzle
into place when He clearly called Tim and I into abortion
recovery ministry full-time.

As the founders of First Step, the revelation that I would
be passing the torch to someone else to lead the organization
was, quite honestly, scary at first. But peace came quickly as
our prayers shifted toward trusting God to bring the right
person to take the reins. After months of fervent prayer, He
provided an amazing woman of God, exploding with gifts and
talents, to bear the title, Executive Director. His timing was
perfect, gracefully releasing me to fulfill my life calling...to
help the sea of women heal from the pain of abortion.

God also made it clear that Tim and I are to engage in
ministry together as a couple.

An incredibly high number of couples who have abortions
together, do not stay together, whether married or not. As
described in our story, abortion creates a massive wedge

between the mother and father, a chasm that, more often than not, ends the relationship.

We thank God for being the glue to hold our relationship together, and for the foundation of covenant we both had regarding marriage in the eyes of God. Through all the ups and downs, twists and turns we experienced the past 35 years, we are blessed to share a relationship that is stronger now than it has ever been. We give God all the glory, honor and praise!

How We Accomplish Our Mission

Debbie

#1 - Speaking

As a restored couple, our primary ministry involves verbally sharing our story openly and transparently. Whether the audience is one or thousands, we honestly proclaim the devastation abortion reeked in our family, and how the transformative power of God brought restoration.

For freedom to become reality for the multitudes, it is imperative that women and men who are set free, rise up and speak out about our struggles and our victories after abortion. Rev. 12:11 says,

> "They overcame him by the blood of the Lamb and by the word of their testimony; they did not love their lives so much as to shrink from death."

We overcome not only by the blood Jesus shed to wipe away our sin and guilt, but by speaking our testimony to others! The more we speak, the more confident and secure we are in our healing.

God also uses our testimonies to guide others toward healing.

Because there is such a negative stigma about abortion, the shame beats us into submissive silence. Abortion proponents sell the lie that abortion is like getting your tooth pulled...no big deal. The lie that it's a woman's right to get an abortion and she knows what is best for her life situation. The lie that there are no ill effects after abortion.

Because we buy the deception they sell, we feel isolated and believe we are the only ones who are struggling.

Everyone says it's no big deal, but I am suffering.

Physically.

Emotionally.

Mentally.

Spiritually.

Relationally.

There must be something wrong with me.

Satan uses his deception to further separate us from truth and help. In that isolation he re-plays the condemning memories over and over in our minds, stripping away our very identity. Our identity becomes the pain we live in.

By men and women speaking out after finding healing through Christ, our words are light to those in darkness, a healing balm to raw wounds, a flicker of hope that healing is possible.

For those who are walking through life after abortion thinking they are OK, a testimony may bring the reality of hidden pain or false beliefs to the forefront, offering the opportunity to address those issues.

Our testimonies also open the eyes of those who have never experienced abortion to get an inside perspective behind the decision and heartbreak, in order to offer grace, love and compassion to those who are hurting, rather than judgment.

How God plans to use our stories to tug on someone's heart is His job. We are simply called to be obedient to share whenever Holy Spirit prompts us and the door is open. The results are in His hands.

#2 - Facilitating Healing Retreats

As described in chapter 13, our ministry includes facilitating healing retreats for small groups of women. Currently, we utilize the Surrendering the Secret Bible study to guide our retreats.

Dedicating 48 hours to attend the retreat, the group commits this time to cocoon away with the Lord, shutting out the distractions of life, intentionally focusing on our relationship with God.

Diving into His word individually and processing it together as a group reveals truth and revelations, destroys the strongholds keeping many of us from walking in freedom, offers us permission to grieve the loss of our child(ren), and honor and celebrate their value.

The transformation that occurs in each participant in just two days is awe-inspiring. Each one enters the retreat as a crushed, wilted flower, then springs to life as a beautiful, vibrant, new creation, free to live life in abundance!

#3 - Writing

For those who may not be ready to personally talk to someone about their abortion experience, the written word extends the opportunity to seek help anonymously...a lifeline of sorts. Suffering men and women are searching for answers from behind the prison walls of abortion, and this book, our blog, or other written materials may be the avenue God uses to empower them with courage to take the next step toward healing…toward the cross. To make that call. To send that email. To join that healing group.

Tim

Our prayer day by day, is to say "Yes, Lord" as we make ourselves available to Him and His Kingdom work. We wake up every day with gratitude and thankfulness knowing exactly what we are called to do. All our decisions are based around doing whatever it takes to stand for life and see others find healing from their abortion experiences.

There is nothing more rewarding than helping someone find the grace and forgiveness and a re-purposed life that only comes from the healing of Jesus Christ and His sacrifice made on our behalf.

Witnessing the transformation from a life of ash into a life of beauty is truly remarkable. I believe as more and more men find freedom from their past abortion experiences and regain their voice to speak and give testimony, it will lead to a great awakening for our families, our cities, our states, our country and ultimately the world!

Some might say or think this is a lofty goal, to believe men will respond and step into Godly leadership just because they confront their abortion trauma. I have experienced it first-hand in my own life and witnessed the transformation in others as well.

We choose daily to trust that the love of God is greater than any force ever. Jesus is the way-maker…He is the chain-breaker. Nothing can defeat or overcome the mighty name of Jesus!

"Do not weep! See, the Lion of the tribe of Judah, the Root of David, has triumphed." Revelation 5:5

We believe the days of men and women weeping and hurting and suffering from their abortion wounds is coming to an end.

We believe God wants to raise up a mighty army to take back what the devil has stolen!

We will stand for what's right and will fight to set the captives free.

Because the Lion of the tribe of Judah, the Root of David has triumphed!

15

Next Step

If you are ready to take the next step toward healing, please reach out to us via our website and explore the life-giving resources listed in the next few pages. We would love to help guide your healing journey.

If you feel compelled to connect with this ministry, to support our mission through prayer, finances, or volunteering, please contact us via our website. We cannot fulfill this mission on our own…it takes teamwork.

For those interested in scheduling us to speak to your church, women's/men's/couples' conference, small group, pro-life event or fundraising banquet, head to our website. We would be honored to engage your group to help accomplish your goals.

www.DebbieAndTimShultz.com

Resources

Surrendering the Secret is an honest, interactive Bible study that will allow women to release the burden of abortion and find freedom through safe community, while experiencing hope and joy, as shame and failure are replaced with beauty. Find more information, join the online community, and locate a group near you at **www.SurrenderingtheSecret.com**.

Silent No More is a campaign where Christians make the public aware of the devastation abortion brings to women and men. It seeks to expose and heal the secrecy and silence surrounding the emotional and physical pain of abortion by encouraging men and women to share their stories. **www.silentnomoreawareness.org**

PATH (Post Abortion Transformation and Healing) is a private Facebook group designed to be a God honoring, safe and confidential place for women who have experienced the guilt, shame and/or regret of a past abortion. It is a place to share personal experiences through the healing process by women who have been through it or are ready to begin their journey.
www.facebook.com/groups/PostAbortionTransformatio nHealing

The Elliot Institute was founded to conduct research and education on the impact of abortion on women, men, siblings, and society, and serves as an advocate to help those seeking help. **www.AfterAbortion.org**

Men & Abortion Network: Reclaiming Fatherhood's mission is "to promote emotional healing for men who have lost a child to abortion, and to create awareness among the counseling community, the pro-life movement and society as a whole regarding the impact of abortion on millions of these hurting fathers. **www.MenAndAbortion.net**

For Pastors & Leaders

"All churches do not have the human resources or the spiritual and psychological skills to meet every need. But, providing a safe place to disclose needs and have them received is a central mandate of the church and the very least we can do." Ken Blue, Healing Spiritual Abuse (IVP, 1993)

A survey conducted by LifeWay Research & commissioned by Care Net reveals some startling statistics about how women who have experienced abortion view the Church. (Source: *https://resources.care-net.org/free-resources/*)

1 in 4 women were attending a Christian Church once a month or more at the time of their first abortion.

As women considered their abortion decision, the most typical reactions/expectations to receive from a local church were **judgmental or condemning**.

Only **7%** stated they were likely to discuss their decision to terminate their pregnancy with someone at a local church.

76% of women indicate local churches had no influence on their decision.

49% of women agree that pastors' teachings on forgiveness don't seem to apply to terminated pregnancies.

More than half of churchgoers who have had an

abortion report that no one at church knows they have had a pregnancy terminated.

This research reveals there are millions of hurting individuals sitting in our church pews every week.

Our passion is to see families, churches and cities transformed through Christ! And to see churches become safe spaces for those making difficult pregnancy decisions, as well as those who have already made regretful decisions and are suffering in silent pain.

We are here to serve the Bride of Christ, to bring awareness about the devastation abortion brings to those inside and outside our church walls, and to empower pastors and leaders to create an environment of love, forgiveness, grace, acceptance, and healing for those struggling after abortion.

As these men and women are finding freedom in Christ, a mighty army is rising up to take back what the enemy has stolen, to be warriors in advancing God's kingdom! An army of individuals ready to serve the Lord wholeheartedly and to their fullest potential!

Is your church a safe place?

Testimonials about Debbie and Tim's Ministry:

"Powerful. Overwhelming. Debbie and Tim tell the story of their struggles with an unplanned pregnancy and subsequent abortion early in their relationship in a way that draws the listener in as if you were alongside them. As their story counties they share the crushing aftereffects of the abortion to them individually as well as to their marriage and family. But the most powerful impact of their testimony is the story of redemption through the powerful forgiveness and grace of God. No one who hears them speak walks away unchanged." - Phil Harris (Banquet attendee)

"I had a chance to hear Debbie's testimony at a Baptist Women's Conference and was impressed with her openness and authenticity. Her willingness to share her story and the work she was doing with pregnant women, gave me the strength to face and admit to my own abortion that occurred over 40 years ago. From that has come complete healing and restoration. I thank God for Debbie!" - Kelley (Women's conference workshop attendee)

"Tim and Debbie have a compelling story and a unique ability to draw you into it. Their passion for life is contagious and their humility inspiring. After hearing them speak, I was inspired to become a volunteer and eventually a board member at First Step Women's Center. No matter how many times I have heard them speak, I always look forward to the next time

I have the opportunity." - Roger Meridith, Pastor, Sherman Church of the Nazarene

"I truly thought I was healed after struggling from a past abortion. I was set free from all my guilt and shame, but I had not validated or celebrated my baby's life until I went through the Surrendering the Secret retreat, with Debbie facilitating. That was the missing piece (peace) of the puzzle. God is never finished with us as long as we are open to His leading. Thank you, Jesus. And thank you Debbie." - Penny

"I came into the retreat seeing myself as a murderer, but left seeing myself as a mother! He showed me what forgiveness truly means and how painful deception is. I am a mother. While never having another child - I am a mother and once had a child." - Val

"God opened my heart and released the burden and secret of carrying all this for 43 years. God loves me and is not disappointed in me. This was the best thing I could have ever done." - Pam

"God allowed me to see the child as a child, and permission to love him. My child still matters to the Lord. The key to healing is receiving God's forgiveness - it was never my job to forgive myself...just receive." - Mary

"I am so thankful that God put Debbie in my life to minister healing to me from a past abortion. Already having had some healing through a church retreat, I thought I was fine. But God used Debbie to show me I was still hurting, and through the Bible study I am now 100% free from the guilt and shame of my past!" - Katie

"God helped me to know that I am not alone. That I no longer am a captive to my shame." - Deb

"Debbie and Tim's ministry was like getting a redo. All of the dead, dry places in my life came back to life!" - Robin

About the Authors

Debbie and Tim Shultz are the Founders of First Step Women's Center in Springfield, IL, where Debbie was the Executive Director from 2007 - 2019.

First Step's mission is to be the first step for women facing unplanned pregnancies, transforming their fear into confidence, and empowering them to make healthy, life-affirming decisions. First Step also acknowledges the devastation abortion causes and the need for abortion recovery ministry.

Debbie has been facilitating abortion recovery groups since 2008 in Illinois and plans to continue this vital ministry in Tennessee. They both love to share their redemption story to individuals or groups of any size, with a passion to help others find the same freedom they have found in Christ.

Debbie and Tim have been married 32 years and are proud parents to five incredible people, along with three bonus kids (their spouses), and four amazing, energetic grandkids (and counting)!

They currently reside in south-central Tennessee, after living in Illinois most of their lives.

Made in the USA
Middletown, DE
09 September 2024

60278099R10077